Tagging

People-Powered Metadata for the **Social Web**

Gene **Smith**

New Riders

VOICES THAT MATTER™

Tagging: People-Powered Metadata for the Social Web
Gene Smith

New Riders
1249 Eighth Street
Berkeley, CA 94710
510/524-2178
510/524-2221 (fax)
Find us on the World Wide Web at: www.peachpit.com
To report errors, please send a note to errata@peachpit.com

New Riders is an imprint of Peachpit, a division of Pearson Education
Copyright © 2008 by Gene Smith

Acquisitions editor: Michael Nolan
Development editor: Box Twelve Communications, Inc.
Production coordinator: Becky Winter
Copyeditor: Kim Wimpsett
Proofreader: Kim Saccio-Kent
Technical editor: Chris Farnum
Compositor: Danielle Foster
Indexer: Karin Arrigoni
Cover design: Mimi Heft
Interior design: Mimi Heft

ISBN 13 978-0-321-52917-6
ISBN 10 0-321-52917-0

9 8 7 6 5 4 3 2 1

Printed and bound in the United States of America

For Jen, Noah, Avery, and Evan.

Acknowledgments

In many ways this book grew out of the conversations and presentations I've shared with friends at information architecture and user experience conferences. Thomas Vander Wal, Rashmi Sinha, Peter Morville, and Peter Merholz come to mind immediately, but there are many others.

I'm grateful to the people I interviewed for this book: James Melzer, Alex Wright, David Weinberger, Tim Spalding, David Millen, Mike Migurski, Peter Van Dijck, and Timo Hannay. Tom Coates, Moritz Stefaner, and Jane Murison generously contributed their work, and I'm honored to have it.

Several people gave me the encouragement I needed to start writing a book: Christina Wodtke, Lou Rosenfeld, and in particular Liz Danzico who read early outlines and connected me with Peachpit. When it came time to start writing, my colleagues at nForm gave me the time and space I needed. Jess McMullin and Yvonne Shek kept our business thriving while I wrote, and, believe me, I'm thankful.

Chris Farnum was the technical editor on this book. If you find errors or omissions, you can bet that Chris tried to get me to fix them. Chapter 7 was improved thanks to the technical expertise of Jonathan Snook and my colleague, Toby Spendiff. Joe Lamantia and Johanna Dietrich also reviewed early drafts and provided excellent suggestions.

The team at Peachpit/New Riders—Michael Nolan, Becky Winter, Cliff Colby, and many others I never met—have been fantastic throughout the project. Jeff Riley brought his considerable experience to this book, and I was happy to have it. He kept me on track and on topic. Thanks, Jeff.

One cold day in 1982 my parents, Ellen and Bob, brought home an Apple II computer. That was a pivotal day. For that, and everything else, thanks.

I also owe a huge thanks to my children, Noah and Avery, for their general inspiration and infectious enthusiasm.

Finally, I would be nowhere without Jen Beverly. She read every chapter, kept me going when I wanted to quit, and let me sleep late after all-night writing sessions. She did it all while pregnant and, later, while tending to our new son, Evan (who was born roughly between Chapters 4 and 5). I couldn't ask for a better partner.

Contents

Introduction

"When the novelty wears off...I think that tagging will have altered the information landscape in a fundamental way."

—Jon Udell

About three years ago I asked a simple question on the Information Architecture Institute's mailing list: "Some of you might have noticed services like Furl, Flickr, and Del.icio.us using user-defined labels or tags to organize and share information.... Is there a name for this kind of informal social classification?" That question started an enduring interest in tags, folksonomies, and other kinds of people-powered metadata.

Tagging *is* changing how we find, use, and share information. And as Jon Udell suggests, it will have a long-term impact on our information landscape.

This book documents those changes. It's a guide to the *what* and *how* (and sometimes *why*) of tagging. As much as possible I tried to use real-world examples and research. You'll find more practical applications here than philosophical implications.

Ultimately, this book exists to help you understand tagging and design tagging systems that work for you and your users. Whether you're a Web designer, developer, information architect, user experience developer, or product manager, you'll find useful concepts and examples in this book. Of course, the book focuses on tagging, but I hope you'll also find the discussions of information architecture, social software, and interface design enlightening and valuable.

Each chapter covers a different aspect of tagging—starting from the most general topics and moving to more specific ones:

- Chapter 1 introduces tagging, outlines the three-part model of tagging systems we'll use throughout the book, and explains why tagging matters.

- Chapter 2 looks at the value of tagging: the return on experience people get from tagging and the return on investment you can expect when building your tagging system.

- In Chapter 3 you'll learn about the architecture of a tagging system. The rules and relationships you define for your system will influence all activity within.

- Tags as metadata is the subject of Chapter 4. You'll learn about folksonomies, as well as approaches that mix tags with taxonomies and other classification systems.

- Chapter 5 discusses navigation and the visualization of tags, including an in-depth look at the now-ubiquitous tag clouds.

- Chapter 6 gives you the lowdown on tagging interfaces. You'll learn about patterns for adding tags, different kinds of suggestions, and features for managing tags.

- In Chapter 7 you'll learn about the technical design of a tagging system. It includes data models, scripts, and other tools to help you implement the ideas found in the rest of the book.

The three appendixes of the book are case studies devoted to particular kinds of tagging applications:

- Appendix A considers tagging in social bookmarking applications. In it you'll find a short (but interesting) history of Del.icio.us, the first collaborative tagging application.

- Appendix B covers media sharing. You'll learn about the similarities—and substantial differences—between Flickr, YouTube, SlideShare, and other media-sharing sites.

- Tagging in personal information management is the subject of Appendix C. It includes examples of Microsoft's Photo Gallery and BlueOrganizer.

Throughout the book I tried to include the best ideas and examples I could find in the most detail space would allow. But Web sites change quickly and frequently. By the time you read this, I expect that a few of the examples used in this book will have already been updated. If you run across a case like this, think of it as an opportunity to compare and contrast how things used to work with how they currently work. Also, drop by my Web site at http://genesmith.ca and let me know so I can keep track of these changes.

1 What Is Tagging?

WHAT YOU'LL LEARN IN THIS CHAPTER:

- A basic model of tagging systems

- Five different kinds of tagging systems

- Where tagging sits between personal information management, information architecture, and social software

Walk into the public library in Danbury, Connecticut, and you'll find the usual shelves stacked with books, organized into neat rows. Works of fiction are grouped alphabetically by the author's last name. Nonfiction titles are placed into their proper Dewey Decimal categories just like they are at tens of thousands of other libraries in North America.

But visit the Danbury Library's online catalog (http://danburylibrary.org), and you'll find something rather unlike a typical library.

A search for *The Catcher in the Rye* brings up not just a call number but also a list of related books and tags—keywords such as "adolescence," "angst," "coming of age," and "New York"—that describe J. D. Salinger's classic novel (see **Figure 1.1**). Click the tag "angst," and you'll find a list of angsty titles such as *The Bell Jar*, *The Stranger*, and *The Virgin Suicides*. If you look up *The Stranger*, you'll find tags such as "existentialism," "philosophy," and "French literature."

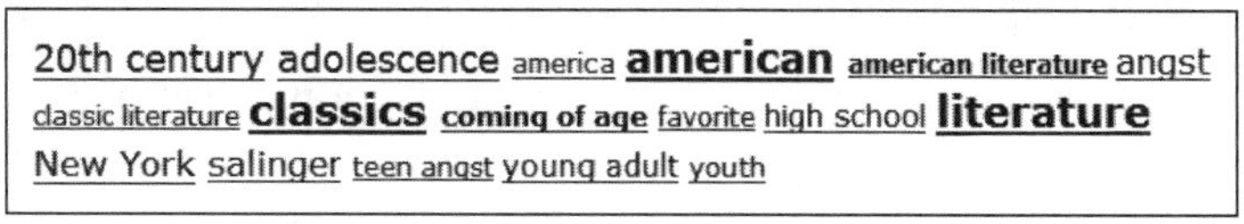

20th century adolescence america **american** american literature angst classic literature **classics** coming of age favorite high school **literature** New York salinger teen angst young adult youth

Figure 1.1 Tags for *The Catcher in the Rye*.

Each tag is a springboard to a new set of books and ideas. Clicking "existentialism" calls up the works of Kafka and Dostoyesvky, while clicking "French literature" brings up Proust, Flaubert, and Dumas. Each tag brings together a collection of books united by a different relationship.

If you find yourself looking at Dumas's *The Count of Monte Cristo*, you might be tempted to explore the tag "revenge." There you'll find Herman Melville's classic *Moby Dick*, Neil Gaiman's graphic novel *The Sandman*, and Olivia Goldsmith's *The First Wives Club*, which is a fine place to start exploring the world of "chick lit." You can continue this process of leapfrogging between tags and books indefinitely.

These tags aren't the work of the diligent librarians in Danbury. They come from LibraryThing (see **Figure 1.2**), a Web site where more than 200,000 book aficionados from all over the world can track and *tag*—add descriptive keywords to—their personal libraries. LibraryThing's members have added nearly 20 million tags to 15 million books, making it the second largest "library" in North America.

Figure 1.2 LibraryThing, a Web site (http://www.librarything.com) where people share their personal book collections.

LibraryThing is one of many Web sites and applications that use *tagging*, an emerging approach to organizing information that uses keywords contributed by ordinary users. Community Libraries like the one in Danbury can access LibraryThing's data to help their patrons discover and explore new books.

How Tagging Works

If you're a book lover, you might sign up for LibraryThing. You'll notice that after you've added a book or two you can also include some words to describe each book.

You add some tags to *Pride and Prejudice*, such as "Jane Austen," "19th century," "English," "fiction," and "romance." You do the same with *Middlemarch*, *Catch-22*, *Mastering Regular Expressions*, *Don't Make Me Think*, and your other favorite books.

You've now done five things:

- First, you've created a way to browse your own collection of books based on your own language and interests. You can tag *Pride and Prejudice* with descriptive terms such as "19th century" and "romance," but you could also use "brooding male protagonist," "happy ending," "gift from Mom," or whatever other language you find useful.

- Second, by assigning multiple tags to the book, you've created multiple ways of finding it. This is, in essence, like putting the same book on two shelves. The next time you look for gifts from your mother, or stories with happy endings, you'll find *Pride and Prejudice*.

- Third, your tags have become part of the community pool of tags for each book. Tagging creates a bridge between personal and community knowledge; everyone's tags together form a kind of community consensus about the book. (It turns out that "19th century" and "romance" are two of the most popular tags for *Pride and Prejudice*.)

- Fourth, your tags are potentially a new way of connecting *Pride and Prejudice* to other books. Or if you've used common tags, you've reinforced the existing connections.

- Finally, your tags are little hooks that can be used to pull together information from other sites that use tags. Content from Technorati, Flickr, Del.icio.us, and other Web 2.0 sites can be aggregated using the tag "romance."

It's the combination of these five features that makes tagging a unique and powerful way of organizing information. In this book, we'll look at how you can use tags to manage your own information. We'll also look at the social side of tagging and how it is being used in online communities.

By the end of the book, you'll understand the ins and outs of designing a tagging system. You'll be able to leverage the expertise of your users through tagging. And you'll pick up a few tips about designing social applications.

Let's get started.

A Basic Model of Tagging Systems

Tagging can be broken down into a fairly simple model where users apply tags to resources such as photos or Web pages within a system (see **Figure 1.3**).

Tagging System

Figure 1.3 In a tagging system, *users* add *tags* to *resources*.

USERS

We'll call the people who employ our tagging system our *users* (occasionally we'll call them *taggers*). They create the tags, and sometimes they add resources.

Our users have a variety of different interests, needs, goals, and motivations. But one thing is certain: they aren't tagging because they think tagging is particularly awesome or fun. They are trying to achieve some larger goal—such as sharing a photo or labeling a document so they can find it later. Tagging helps them accomplish this.

RESOURCES

Resources are the items that users tag. A resource can be just about anything—a book, a Web page, a video, or even a location. As long as we have a way to uniquely identify something, it can be tagged.

Within each tagging system, resources often share some common properties. In LibraryThing, the resources are books. At the photo-sharing site Flickr (http:// flickr.com), the resources are photos.

TAGS

The keywords added by users are *tags*. Because tagging is open-ended, tags can be just about any kind of term. They can be descriptions of the resource's subject matter, its location, its intended use, a reminder, or something else entirely. They can be individual words such as "funny" or phrases such as "gift from mom." Different people have different tagging patterns—some people's tags are more expressive, while others are merely descriptive. Tagging systems allow for—and even encourage—these differences.

Tags are essentially *metadata* about the resource. According to the National Information Standards Organization (NISO), metadata is "structured information that describes, explains, locates, or otherwise makes it easier to retrieve, use, or manage an information resource." In other words, tags are information about information. We'll spend Chapter 4 talking about tags as metadata.

Introducing Tag Clouds

A *tag cloud* is a method of presenting tags where the more frequently used tags are emphasized—usually in size or color. Tag clouds tell you at a glance which tags are more popular. In **Figure 1.4**, "book" and "christianity" are more popular than "art." Because each tag is also a link, the tag cloud is also a form of navigation.

art baby bards and minstrels bible biography blu-ray blues book business camera canon cd children childrens books christian christianity christmas classic classic rock comedy comics cookbook cooking

Figure 1.4 A tag cloud from Amazon.com

THE TAGGING SYSTEM

All tagging happens in the context of a system, and the system defines what kind of tagging can take place. For example, the system may allow users to add their own resources, or it might restrict them to tagging existing resources. The system might allow users to tag any resource, or it might limit them to tagging their own.

Even though tagging systems generally give users the freedom to use whatever terms they want, the system might forbid certain kinds of tags. Amazon.com, for example, won't allow objectionable words as tags.

In other words, the system contains the rules about who can tag, what can be tagged, and what kind of tags can be used.

Today's Tagging Systems

In this book, we'll talk a lot about *tagging systems*. This is a helpful, if imprecise, term for Web sites and applications that use some form of tagging.

At its most basic level, tagging is a feature that makes these Web sites more useful. Tagging, on its own, is like a card catalog without a library of books. Or it's like a file system without any files. Tagging needs users and resources to be useful.

We'll use the phrase *tagging system* in a holistic way that refers to the tagging application itself, the people who use it, the resources and tags it contains, and the kinds of interactions it supports. This big-picture view will help us remember that tags are more than just metadata in an application. They're a tool people use to track, share, and find information.

Most Web sites that use tagging fall into one of five basic categories. Let's look at some examples in each category.

MANAGING PERSONAL INFORMATION

One of tagging's main benefits is that it lets you organize information in your own way. With Google's popular e-mail program, Gmail, you can tag your e-mail. In Gmail tags are called *labels*, but the concept is the same. You can apply several labels to an e-mail and then filter your messages by the labels. If you used folders, you would have to move every message to a single location. With labels, you can find your e-mail in two or more places at once.

Photo Gallery, a photo management application that comes with the Microsoft Windows Vista operating system, gives you a flexible tagging system for your digital photos. Photo Gallery was designed help you manage thousands, or even tens of thousands, of photos. (We look at Photo Gallery's tagging in Appendix C.)

SOCIAL BOOKMARKING

Users of social bookmarking Web sites submit, share, and tag Web pages with other users. Most social bookmarking Web sites offer the same core set of features: you post links, comment on them, and add tags. Your links and tags become part of the community pool, and they are available to other users to browse.

In addition to helping you find your bookmarks, tags also serve as a kind of vote on the subject matter of the bookmark. If most people tag a page as "javascript" and "tutorial," you can be confident that the page offers an introduction to JavaScript. As you'll see in later chapters, there are many interesting statistical patterns in the tags from social bookmarking services.

Del.icio.us was the first social bookmarking service and the first Web site to employ social tagging. It now has dozens—if not hundreds—of competitors.

Ma.gnolia (http://ma.gnolia.com/popular) is one of those competitors (see **Figure 1.5**). There are even social bookmarking niches. CiteULike and Connotea, for example, are aimed at academics.

Figure 1.5 The social bookmarking site Ma.gnolia.

COLLECTING AND SHARING DIGITAL OBJECTS

In the past few years we've seen an explosion of Web sites designed for collecting, organizing, sharing, and tagging digital objects. These objects could be photos, documents, presentations, videos, or just about anything else that can be represented digitally.

Flickr (http://flickr.com), the popular photo-sharing site, was one of the first to implement tags (see **Figure 1.6**). Dozens of applications have followed Flickr's lead. SlideShare, for example, lets you share (and tag) Microsoft Office PowerPoint presentations. LibraryThing's users share their personal book collections, while YouTube users tag the videos they upload.

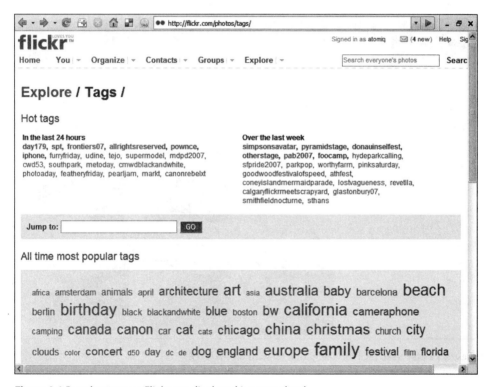

Figure 1.6 Popular tags on Flickr are displayed in a tag cloud.

IMPROVING THE E-COMMERCE EXPERIENCE

Online stores have traditionally separated their wares into hierarchical categories, but several are now starting to experiment with tagging. Tagging has the potential to improve the "findability" of products through search and navigation.

Etsy (http://www.etsy.com), an online store that sells one-of-a-kind craft items, generates part of its site navigation based on tags submitted by users (see **Figure 1.7**). This lets the navigation change based on the kinds of items people are submitting to sell on the site.

Figure 1.7 Etsy uses tags for navigation (shown on the left).

Buzzillions.com (http://www.buzzillions.com) offers product reviews where people tag products with "pros," "cons," and "good for..." (see **Figure 1.8**). Buzzillions.com reviews are more structured than typical product reviews, which can help people evaluate a product quickly. Because they use tagging, the reviews are also quite flexible. You can, for example, tag your new running shoes with qualities that are meaningful to you.

Figure 1.8 Product reviews on Buzzillions.

Finally, tagging on e-commerce sites can be used to help grow a community. Amazon.com, for example, has "customer communities" based on the tags people use on their products.

OTHER USES

Designers and developers are finding new uses for tagging all the time. One intriguing example is the ESP Game.

The ESP Game pairs two anonymous Web users and asks them to look at a photo and think up tags for it. The goal of the game is for both players to agree on one or more tags for that photo. When they agree on a tag, they get points. The idea behind the ESP Game is that if two independent and anonymous people can agree on a tag for a photo, then there's a good chance that tag will accurately describe the photo. If you play this game over hundreds or thousands of rounds, you'll come up with pretty good metadata for those photos.

Another innovative use of tagging comes from Wesabe, a personal finance Web site, where you can tag your financial transactions. Wesabe analyzes tagging patterns to come up with recommendations for merchants. Thus, if you made a purchase at Starbucks, you might see the "coffee" or "food" as suggestions based on the tags of other Wesabe users.

Finally, blogging tools such as WordPress use tags so users have a quick and easy way to categorize their posts. These tags are picked up by blog aggregators such as Technorati, which uses them to discover trends across the blogosphere. At the end of the book you'll find case studies on three kinds of tagging systems: social bookmarking, personal information management, and media sharing.

Three Perspectives on Tagging

Tagging sits at the intersection of three established fields (see **Figure 1.9**):

■ Information architecture

■ Social software

■ Personal information management (PIM)

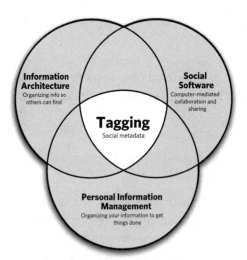

Figure 1.9 Much of the interest in tagging is because of the way it bridges personal information management, information architecture, and social software.

Like many other disciplines, these three have their frames of reference through which they view the world.

INFORMATION ARCHITECTURE

The Information Architecture Institute defines *information architecture* as "the structural design of shared information environments" and "the art and science of organizing and labeling Web sites, intranets, online communities, and software to support usability and findability."

Information architects are often tasked with developing organizational schemes that work for a diverse population of users—such as document repositories, corporate intranets, or large-scale Web sites. They're concerned about how people find and use information across a variety of scenarios. Information architects have focused on using controlled vocabularies, search-and-browse systems, and consistent navigation schemes to achieve this success.

SOCIAL SOFTWARE

Social software has a variety of definitions, ranging from the clinical ("software that enables people to connect through computer-mediated communication") to the pragmatic ("stuff that gets spammed"). We can think of social software as applications that people use to communicate, collaborate, and share online.

The people who design social software are interested in facilitating group interaction within the system. They often delight in unanticipated uses of a social application. (Of course, it's important for people to be able to find and use information in social software systems too.)

PERSONAL INFORMATION MANAGEMENT

According to Wikipedia, *personal information management* "refers to both the practice and the study of the activities people perform in order to acquire, organize, maintain, retrieve, and use information items such as documents (paper-based and digital), Web pages, and e-mail messages for everyday use to complete tasks (work-related and not) and fulfill a person's various roles (as parent, employee, friend, member of community, etc.)."

In the world of PIM, what's good is what works for you. There are popular computer programs for managing information and methods for keeping yourself on track (David Allen's book *Getting Things Done: The Art of Stress-Free Productivity* is a hit with the Web design crowd). These systems help you file, track, and find your information when you need it.

Note

Christopher Allen's "Tracing the Evolution of Social Software" is an excellent history of the key ideas of social software (http://www.lifewithalacrity.com /2004/10/tracing_the_evo.html). For more about information architecture, visit the Information Architecture Institute (http://iainstitute.org).

UNDERSTANDING TAGGING'S TENSION POINTS

The social bookmarking site Del.icio.us introduced the first widely used collaborative tagging system in 2003. As Del.icio.us—and tagging—grew in popularity, it also revealed that there was considerable friction between these three disciplines.

The information architects first noticed that Del.icio.us tags were creating something like the controlled vocabularies they normally created. These *folksonomies* (as they were called) weren't crafted by professionals; they were simply a serendipitous spin-off benefit of people tagging bookmarks for their own personal use.

Many social software folks saw this low-cost metadata, provided by ordinary people, as a way to circumvent more expensive professional metadata creation practices. In many ways, Google—which leveraged the link structure inherent in the Web to build a better search engine—offered a positive example.

In addition to providing cheap metadata, tagging seemed to democratize the process of classification. It took classification away from central authorities (such as librarians and information architects) and gave it back to the people.

Information architect Lou Rosenfeld noticed that tagging isn't all that good at the things information architecture is supposed to do. It doesn't, for example, "support searching and other types of browsing nearly as well as...controlled vocabularies applied by professionals." Others, such as social software guru Clay Shirky, argued that tagging is more cost-effective and less prone to bureaucratic biases than centrally controlled classification systems.

FOUR TENSION POINTS

This friction led to a number of interesting and occasionally heated debates between proponents of different disciplines (discussed in more depth in Chapter 4).

On the surface these debates suggest that there is a fundamental disagreement over what tagging is and what it's good for. At a deeper level, however, it seems obvious that people with different frames of reference on the purpose, economics, and value of classification systems have different perspectives on tagging.

These different perspectives illustrate the *tension points*—where two aspects of tagging seem to be pulling in opposite directions—that exist in tagging systems. These tensions between sociality, idiosyncrasy, control, and expertise permeate many conversations on tagging (see **Table 1.1**).

Throughout the book, in virtually every discussion of design choices or trade-offs, you'll recognize one or more of these tensions.

Table 1.1 Four Tension Points in Tagging Systems

Tension Between...

Personal ← → Social	Do people tag primarily for their own benefit? Or are they motivated by the desire to share information with a group, by the desire to be seen as knowledgeable, or by other social factors?
Idiosyncratic ← → Standard	Should tags be completely unique and idiosyncratic? Or should they be standardized so that they can be used for browsing and searching?
Freedom ← → Control	Does the system give users complete freedom? Or does it influence or control their tags (by offering suggestions, for example)?
Amateur ← → Expert	How qualified are the people tagging? Should tags contributed by amateurs count as much as tags created by experts? How do you reconcile popular opinion expressed through tags with expert opinions when they disagree?

Generally, tagging systems with a social component have more of these tensions than completely private systems. For example:

- Tags in Gmail can be completely personal and idiosyncratic because they're never shared with other users.

- Del.icio.us allows uniquely personal tags (see **Figure 1.10**), but because it's a social application—tags can be used to discover new bookmarks and other users—people often use some common tags.

- Amazon.com's tagging interface guides its users toward popular tags and restricts certain tag choices.

- LibraryThing permits tagging idiosyncrasies but removes personal tags from its LibraryThing for Libraries service.

```
244  curious
 36  custom
  5  ddoi
247  deezine
  4  del.icio.us
  5  demise
  1  detroit
 19  digg
  2  disingenous
  1  distillery
 24  distracto
  1  diy
 36  domesticarts
  1  doodleart
 25  drawn
 11  drink
  6  dublin
 11  dubya
  1  eboy
  1  editor
  2  election
  2  elections
  1  elephantintheroom
```

Figure 1.10 One user's unique tags in Del.icio.us.

One of the goals of this book is to help you understand these tension points and the design trade-offs they bring. Through the examples and case studies you'll see how different tagging systems have dealt with these issues. And you'll come to appreciate that a tagging system that works in one context may not work in another.

Why Tagging Matters

Humans are organizing machines. Our earliest forms of writing were metadata—accounts of livestock, stored food, tributes, and other goods etched onto clay tablets. And since then we've been grouping, sorting, tracking, and organizing just about everything we encounter.

We've also gotten consistently better at organizing things. Today we think nothing of searching the tens of billions of pages that are crawled, indexed, and organized by search engines.

But our information landscape is much different now than it was even five years ago, and tagging heralds some fundamental changes in how we manage information. These changes are partly due to the information explosion we've been experiencing and the need for tools that are purpose-built for our new always-on ubiquitous information environment.

These changes are also happening because our information systems and classification systems are increasingly social systems as well. And they're happening because of changing attitudes about the Web and the emergence of a generation that has never been without the Web.

Alex Wright: Is Tagging an Evolution or a Revolution?

 Alex Wright is a writer and information architect who lives in New York City. He is the author of *Glut: Mastering Information Through the Ages.* He has this to say about tagging:

"There has been no shortage of overblown rhetoric about the tagging phenomenon. Some writers have suggested that it's a kind of epistemological revolution that will change the shape of human knowledge by liberating the practice of classification from old institutional confines and giving (like they used to say) power to the people.

"But people have been classifying things for a long time. The first taxonomies weren't created in libraries or biology labs; they were created by our distant ancestors living in tribal communities tens of thousands of years ago. The earliest 'folk taxonomies' gave people a framework for organizing information about the world around them: plants, animals, weather patterns, and other natural phenomenon. These systems were generated from the bottom up by generations of individuals pooling their knowledge over time. And these systems eventually became remarkably sophisticated: with hierarchical categorization schemes, binomial naming conventions, and many of the basic characteristics of so-called modern taxonomies. Although these systems were rarely written down, they became embedded in human language and deeply entwined with the culture as a whole.

"To understand the importance of tagging, we need to look at it not just in terms of the recent history of institutional classification but also in terms of the reemergence of oral culture online. The linguist Walter J. Ong coined the term *secondary orality* to describe the way electronic media seems to give rise to new modes of communication that have more in common with ancient oral cultures than with more recent, literate forms of writing. Tagging seems to take place right at the crux of these two cultures. On the one hand, it has a literate dimension—meaning gets ascribed and fixed as part of a written public record. At the same time, the underlying process is quite conversational.

"So if we look at tagging not just as a populist alternative to institutional classification but as part of the reemergence of ancient cultural impulses, then perhaps we can understand it as both a revolution and an evolution at the same time."

It's Popular

According to recent research, millions of Americans are tagging every day. A study released by the Pew Internet & American Life Project in January 2007 found that nearly one third of U.S. Internet users, or about 42 million Americans, had tagged some form of online content. About 10 million Americans (7 percent of Internet users) are tagging daily.

These numbers seem huge. And the report itself acknowledges that there's ambiguity around what tagging is. Nonetheless, as the first real study looking at tagging, it shows that people are engaged in tagging in significant numbers.

Taggers resemble other early adopters of technology, according to the Pew report. They tend to be younger; they tend to be more affluent; and more than half have attended college. Interestingly, nearly two-thirds of taggers are African American or Hispanic. The demographic profile of taggers will certainly evolve over time.

Because of the demand created by these early adopters, many more desktop and Web applications support tagging. Today, practically anyone who uses a computer or the Internet is exposed to tagging in some way.

It's Multifaceted

Tags are the first significant change from the one-thing-in-one-place folder metaphor we experience on our computer hard drives and in real life. With tags, your files and photos can be in two, three, or more "places" at once.

This idea may seem unusual if you're comfortable with folders, but it won't for long. As journalist Jon Udell says, "That magical same-thing-in-two-places property may seem less magical to the majority of folks who don't know what I know about directory structures on disks."

As tagging grows in popularity, the idea that the same thing can exist in multiple places will be the norm.

It's Social

The social aspects of tagging are arguably the most interesting.

Del.icio.us introduced the idea that classification could simultaneously be a personal and collaborative process. This is, in fact, a significant change from the past where classification systems—from the Library of Congress right down to the navigation labels for a Web site—were centralized. Del.icio.us also upset the widely held belief that centralization and control went hand in hand with utility.

Librarians, information architects, developers, and other professionals who create classification systems are quick to point out that they have always consulted their users and considered the overall usability of their systems. Fair enough.

What makes tagging different is that every user is helping to shape a consensus around the content of the thing that's being tagged. Tags allow individuals to describe a resource in their own way. Through the most popular tags, we can see a kind of rough consensus on the subject of the resource. But tags also allow minority viewpoints to emerge, even if they never become popular. Everyone's perspective is counted.

This isn't to suggest that you should think about tagging as a replacement for other kinds of categorization or Web site navigation. I'll spend Chapter 4 discussing how tags can complement other classification systems.

It's Flexible

Over time all communities develop their own vocabularies to describe their members, their concerns, and their activities. The online communities that have flourished on the Web are no different. The blogosphere, for example, gives us a steady stream of neologisms (including words such as *blogosphere*).

For many organizations, there's a tension between their own vocabulary and those of their staff, customers, or stakeholders. Tagging offers organizations a way to learn, understand, and adopt the vocabulary of their communities.

It's Ready for the Stream

"The stream" is a metaphor for our new information environment, one where we are immersed in a continual flow of data. The stream consists of photos from your Facebook and Flickr friends, links from Del.icio.us, e-mails entering your inbox, RSS feeds flowing into your feed reader, Twitter tweets, SMS and instant messages, and any other kind of communication or notification you experience every day. It's all the information in your environment continually competing for your attention and action.

Some of the information in your stream is worth reading, saving, or sharing. You could try to maintain some predefined organizational scheme—trying to anticipate all the different kinds of information you'll encounter—but that seems like a losing proposition. The stream moves too quickly. In the stream it's much easier to create categories on the fly.

This is where tagging comes in. Tagging is ready to help you make sense of your stream by giving you maximum organizational power with minimal cognitive overhead.

By being fast, flexible, and simple, tagging is ideally suited for a current of information. It's ready for the stream.

Proto-tags: eBay's Auction Acronyms

eBay has always maintained a large set of categories for its auctions, but buyers and sellers often need a vocabulary to describe their auctions that's outside eBay's official categories. Over time the eBay community evolved a set of acronyms or short words to help further classify their auctions. Here are some examples:

- NWT (new with tags) is mainly used for clothing auctions to indicate the garment has its original tags.

- VHTF (very hard to find) helps you understand how rare collectibles are.

- NRFB (never removed from box) tells you that the original packaging is intact.

- MIJ (made in Japan) tells you the country of origin, which is helpful for items such as electronics.

These proto-tags are added to the auction listing title so other users can easily search or scan for auctions in which they're interested. Despite being widely used, these acronyms have never found their way into eBay's official category system. You can find a complete list of acronyms at http://pages.ebay.com/help/newtoebay/acronyms.html.

Summary

- Tagging is when users apply keyword metadata—or *tags*—to resources such as photos or Web pages within a system.

- Tagging sits at the intersection of three important fields: information architecture, social software, and personal information management.

- Recent debates on tagging illustrate the tension points in most tagging systems—personal versus social uses, individual versus standard tags, freedom versus control, and amateur opinions versus those of experts.

- Tagging matters because it's popular, multifaceted, flexible, and social. It's also made for the stream—the constant flow of information we experience online.

2 The Value of Tagging

WHAT YOU'LL LEARN IN THIS CHAPTER:

■ Balancing return on experience and return on investment in a tagging system

■ Five motivations for people who tag

■ Seven potential benefits for organizations that implement tagging

In roughly three years, tagging went from being a feature on a simple link-sharing Web site to a must-have feature for every new Web application. Why did, as one journalist put it, tag mania sweep the Web?

The answer lies partly in the open-ended nature of tagging—it can be many things to many people. Tagging also helps solve that perennial problem of the Internet age—keeping track of all the links—while enabling a low-threshold form of social engagement.

In this chapter, we'll explore the reasons people tag and discuss some of the benefits they get from tagging. We'll also consider the other side: the owner of the tagging system and what they get from building a tagging system.

What Tags Can Do for You

In the previous chapter, we looked at some examples of tagging along with some reasons why tagging is an important trend. Let's start to articulate the benefits that people get from tagging—from the perspective of the user as well as the creator of the tagging system. We'll use the value-centered design model created by my business partner, Jess McMullin, as the starting point for this discussion.

Value-centered design is based on a simple idea: value comes from balancing the goals of the people who create the system with those of the people who use the system (see **Figure 2.1**). In this section, we'll consider the *return on experience* that users get from tagging as well as the *return on investment* that organizations can receive from implementing tagging.

System Goals

What does the person or organization that creates the tagging system get out of it?

Return on Investment

VALUE

Return on Experience

User Goals

What does the person who uses the tagging system get out of it?

Figure 2.1 The value of your tagging system will come from balancing your user's goals and the system's goals (based on Jess McMullin's Value-Centered Design model).

In this context, *system* refers to your tagging system. You might have several goals depending on why you're building a tagging system and who you're doing it for. You might be adding tagging to a Web site or an intranet, or you might be using it in a consumer Web application. In either case, you need to think about the value you'll get out of tagging (if only to justify the time and money you'll spend developing it).

There's another not-so-subtle reason to talk about system goals. Now that tagging has swept through the commercial Web—and it's no longer considered an innovation—there's increasing interest in large corporations, public sector institutions, and software makers. These organizations, quite rightly, want to know what tagging can do for them. So, it only makes sense to consider return on experience and return on investment at the same time.

Return on Experience: Five Motivations for Tagging

Let's look at five reasons people might gravitate to using tags. These motivations aren't particular to the kind of information being tagged—they just describe the value most people get from tagging. Based on the tagging patterns and applications we've seen, these five motivations are reasonably complete. But they can't be considered exhaustive.

Note

These categories are adapted from the paper "Position Paper, Tagging, Taxonomy, Flickr, Article, ToRead" by Cameron Marlow, Mor Naaman, danah boyd, and Marc Davis. It's available at http://www.semanticmetadata.net/ hosted/taggingws-www2006-files/29.pdf.

Ease of Use

Perhaps the strongest motivation for using tags is they're easy. Adding them requires a minimal investment of time and attention.

There are four main reasons why tags are easy to use.

TAGS ARE SIMPLE

When it comes to interfaces for organizing information, tags are as simple as it gets: you type a few words, and you're done. And instead of creating folders and click-dragging files around, you create multiple paths back to your resources by adding more than one tag.

TAGS ARE FLEXIBLE

Tags also are adaptable to just about any situation, any purpose, and any kind of information. They can be used to describe your feelings, to keep track of news stories for later reading, and to describe the subject of an article. You might tag interesting blog posts with "*****", a video clip as "funny," and a recipe with the name of a complementary wine. If you're an advanced user, you might even create machine tags that can be read by computer programs (more on that in Chapter 7, "Technical Design"). Tags can be whatever you need them to be.

TAGS ARE EXTENSIBLE

One of the joys of tagging is that you never have to click a "Make a New Tag" button. When you need a new tag to describe something, you just type it. Your list of tags can grow as much as you'd like. And the tags you've used before never restrict you. In other words, tags are extensible.

TAGS CAN BE AGGREGATED

Unlike folders, which provide a location for information, tags act as hooks. Disparate bits of content—whether they're created by you or by others—can be connected and aggregated with these identifiers.

Within a site or application, tags can provide a way for people to discover other users with similar interests. When combined with the APIs and data feeds used by many Web 2.0 applications, tags can be used to bring together information across multiple Web sites.

AND ONE CAVEAT

There are, of course, cases where tagging doesn't work as well as we might like. Not every application, intranet, or Web site is well suited to tagging. Not every user wants tags. The tags themselves can be messy and may not conform to any recognizable pattern. And what one tag means over here might be something completely different over there. We'll discuss all of these challenges, but they don't diminish the simple utility of tagging.

Managing Personal Information

Now that we've established that tags are easy to use, the next question is "What do we use them for?" The most obvious application is to let you track and organize different things so you can find them again when you need them.

We've always had folders for filing our documents—digital and physical. Folders bring many benefits, but they often limit us to putting one thing in one place. Even our computers, which aren't limited by the constraints of the physical world, make it surprisingly difficult to put the same thing in two places.

According to Rashmi Sinha, social media consultant and CEO of SlideShare, there are three main reasons tagging can be easier than a categorization scheme created with one-thing-in-one-place folders:

- You don't need to consider the whole categorization scheme. You can just add the tags that seem appropriate.

- You can add any tags you want, instead of finding the one category that's the best fit.

- Recategorization is easy if we make a mistake (or if the world changes so that our categories no longer fit).

Despite these advantages, personal information management (PIM) is often more complex than just putting files in the right place.

TAGS AND FOLDERS: KEY DIFFERENCES

Research shows that people rely on folders for more than just storing documents. Creating and nesting folders can be part of a divide-and-conquer strategy people use to complete their personal projects. Some people even *hack* their folders—prefixing them with numbers or letters—to ensure the folders are ordered in the right way.

Folder structures capture important information about projects, processes, and the domain of work—in addition to storing documents. As one researcher says, "Folders may represent, if only crudely, a person's emerging, often hard-won, understanding of the information items contained within, their relationships to each other, their important properties."

Nonetheless, several studies reveal that people are often inconsistent and irrational when it comes to managing their personal information. Letters, for example, are often treated with special attention, while bookmarks or e-mail are left untended. Maintaining collections of personal information is also not a high priority for users. Participants in one study said they would rather search for a Web site they had saved than look through their bookmarks list—but they would still bookmark Web pages.

You can probably expect people to bring those inconsistencies to tagging as well. So instead of re-finding information through their tags, they'll simply search for it. They may never re-tag resources, just like they don't organize their browser bookmarks.

But if life online means we're immersed in a continual stream of new information, then tagging can be a viable and valuable solution to people's PIM problems. The fluidity of tags—where new categories can emerge with a few keystrokes and old categories can fade away simply through benign neglect—can be an advantage for people who just want to keep up with their daily deluge of information.

Note

An excellent source of research and information on personal information management is the Keeping Found Things Found project at the University of Washington (http://kftf.ischool.washington.edu/).

A Brief History of Folders

Ever wonder how folders became our main tool for organizing files on computers? It started with the desktop metaphor, which aimed to hide esoteric command-line instructions with graphical objects that would be familiar to the office workers of the time—such as folders, filing cabinets, an inbox, and trash cans. The Apple Macintosh was the first popular computer to use the desktop metaphor.

But folders themselves—the slabs of manila cardstock you stack on your desk—were part of a 19th-century information revolution called *vertical filing*. Before vertical filing, people would use antiquated methods such as pigeonhole cabinets, ledger books, or flat stacks to store their documents.

Inventors in the late 19th century developed a number of innovations to make filing more efficient. But it was the Library Bureau—founded by librarian Melvil Dewey—that put together the winning combination of vertical filing cabinets and cardstock folders.

Compared to pigeonhole cabinets or ledger books, vertical filing was fast, flexible, scalable, and much more efficient. Vertical files held as much as 10 times more than flat files or box files.

Vertical filing was introduced at the 1893 World's Fair in Chicago where it won a gold medal. Within 20 years most American businesses were using vertical filing. And those that keep paper records still do.

Collaborating and Sharing

Sure, tags can be effective as a personal information management tool, but they also provide the foundation for a simple yet robust kind of *social* information management.

In the most popular tagging systems, the social rewards are as meaningful as the personal ones. Participating in a community, sharing our interests, and contributing to the collective good are all fundamentally human motivations, and social tagging systems certainly tap into those. But tagging also offers a passive social component that lets you participate, share, and contribute without actively engaging with other users. Rashmi Sinha calls this *social hum* and likens it to working in a café just to be around people.

There are several reasons you might want to "be around people" in a tagging system:

- In social bookmarking applications, other users might post links that you find interesting.

- You can explore topics using the tags of other users.

- Tag recommendations will be better if other users are sharing the system (in many tagging systems, tag recommendations wouldn't be possible without the contributions of other users).

- Other users might be experts, letting you draft behind them by copying their links and tags.

- You might use tags to connect with other users who have shared interests.

In some cases, tags enable communities of interest to spring up spontaneously.

SEEDING COMMUNITIES

Consider, for example, the use of the tag "nptech"—which stands for *nonprofit tech*—on Del.icio.us. The tag was first used by a small group of technology bloggers but quickly expanded to include others who were interested in using technology to help nonprofit groups.

One frequent user of the tag, Chris Blow, blogged about how "nptech" became the seed for an online community:

> "While I have a 'curmudgeonly' eye for Web 2.0 gizmos, in addition to a deep distrust of technophilic "progress"...I think that the development of this tag is arguably the single largest reason for the current (thriving I think) state of what is commonly called the 'nptech community.' Which means a lot to me."

The community couldn't have come about without people who were passionate about the topic. But the tag—acting as a way to aggregate disparate conversations about the topic—allowed the community to take root.

And that makes it a good example of another social phenomenon common in tagging systems: social proof.

SOCIAL PROOF—OR THE BANDWAGON EFFECT

In many social situations, people will follow the lead of others, assuming they are an expert or just that they have more information. Psychologist Robert Cialdini calls this *social proof*. A classic example of social proof is the canned laughter used in TV sitcoms. Even though people will tell you they dislike it, they laugh longer and harder when it's used.

According to Cialdini, "One means we use to determine what is correct is to find out what other people think is correct. … We view a behavior as more correct in a given situation to the degree that we see others performing it."

In a tagging system, social proof means that some users may be inclined to copy other people's tags instead of adding their own. Sometimes this can reduce the diversity of tags in the system and reinforce the opinions of the early users. In other cases, it can encourage users to gather around a topic and start a community.

Note

For more information on social proof, see Robert Cialdini's book Influence: Science and Practice.

Having Fun

With every social technology comes new forms of play, and tagging is no different.

On Flickr, for example, hundreds of people play the game Squared Circle. The rules are simple: you take a photo of a round object and crop it so that the object is centered in a square frame. Then you post it to Flickr and tag it with "squaredcircle" (see **Figure 2.2**). Through the magic of tags, your photo becomes part of a worldwide pool of photos of round objects in a square frame.

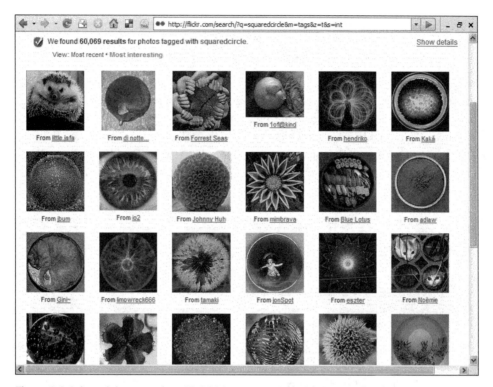

Figure 2.2 A few of the more than 60,000 images tagged with "squaredcircle" on Flickr.

There is no official rule book for Squared Circle. The game emerged, organically, from people posting their often-striking "squaredcircle" photos to Flickr.

Tags provide a simple mechanism for tying together these photos. And once you've added a photo, you're connected with other Squared Circle players (and followers).

Expressing Yourself

Tagging allows you to express your opinion about content and make your judgments, opinions, and identity part of the system.

In social tagging systems, some tags serve a dual purpose. Take the tag "funny," for instance. When you use it, you've created a way to re-find something you thought was funny. But you're also telling other users of the system about what you find humorous, and you're communicating something about who you are.

At the music-sharing site Last.fm, many people use the tag "seen live" to identify the artists they've seen and, presumably, to tell other users who they've seen as well. It's like the online version of wearing the T-shirt you bought at the gig.

Activists have also used tags as their means of expression, creating a new kind of metadata-driven political speech. The Free Software Foundation, for example, launched a tagging campaign on Amazon.com that encouraged people to tag products that used digital rights management software with "defectivebydesign." More than 1,000 people have used the tag on a variety of products, including MP3 players, DVDs, and video game systems. It remains one of the more popular tags on Amazon.com (see **Figure 2.3**).

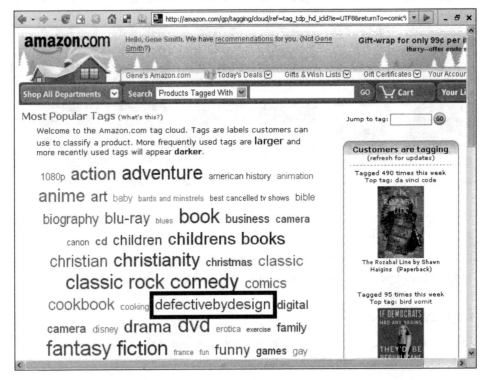

Figure 2.3 The tag "defectivebydesign," part of an anti-DRM campaign, is one of the more popular tags on Amazon.com.

Return on Investment: Seven Business Benefits

Let's turn now to the other side of the value-centered design equation: return on investment. Whether you're a Fortune 500 company managing a localized intranet or a small start-up working on a Web application, you'll want to know the answer to one important question: "What can tagging do for me?"

There are seven potential benefits for organizations that adopt tagging. Some groups may realize many of these, some only one. The key is to understand the possible benefits to you and to design a tagging system that achieves them.

Facilitating Collaboration

Tagging can be a way for users to contribute their knowledge—in the form of resources and tags—to a communal pool.

In their simplest form, social tagging systems allow people to share ideas and resources through passive collaboration. By adding resources and tags to the system, users are helping to build a knowledge base that benefits every other user.

Tags also provide a simple way to capture people's knowledge and terminology. Although some knowledge management efforts explicitly try to identify an organization's experts, tagging systems allow people's expertise to be revealed organically through their contributions.

Obtaining Descriptive Metadata

The traditional way of getting quality metadata involves hiring people such as librarians or indexers to review each resource in a collection and add keywords to it. This can be expensive and time-consuming (though you would typically get high-quality results). You could opt for autoclassification software that extracts keywords from your resources. This method is faster but can also be expensive.

Tagging lets you enlist your users in the metadata creation process, effectively giving you keywords at a very low cost. This approach can be incredibly valuable for photos, videos, and other media that don't have text metadata natively. Tags added to photos in Flickr, for example, help make it easier to find photos through search.

Tag metadata might also be used to identify new keywords that could improve search engine rankings or Web site navigation. If someone tags a Web page with "progressive rock," we can assume they might also use the term "progressive rock" to look for that page in a search engine or menu bar. The page's author can then include the term (if it's relevant) to make the page easier to find.

You should remember, though, that the open-ended nature of tagging systems means you'll probably get some tags that are meaningful only to the person who added them. In Chapter 1, we talked about LibraryThing for Libraries—a service that adds user-generated tags to a library's online catalog. LibraryThing removes personal tags—tags such as "toread" or "did not finish"—from this service.

Enhancing Findability

Tagging can make information easier to find. In social bookmarking systems, for example, tags provide supplemental navigation for users. Each tag is another possible doorway to a resource or a jumping-off point to find related tags.

In some cases, tags can even improve search. Yahoo's MyWeb 2.0, a social bookmark-ing tool similar to Del.icio.us, leverages people's tags to provide them with more rel-evant search results. A more thorough discussion of tags as navigation is coming up in Chapter 5, as well as in the social bookmarking case study in Appendix A.

Increasing Participation

In social tagging systems, adding tags is a low-risk form of participation that may lead people to higher-value contributions.

When the BBC redesigned its regional message boards in 2005, it found that many users were intimidated by the idea of posting to an online forum. Moving from lurker to participant was a major leap. The BBC also discovered that people had difficulty finding relevant content on their message boards because the official topic of a con-versation could be significantly different from the comments added by users.

So the BBC added tagging as part of a strategy to give people low-risk forms of par-ticipation (see **Figure 2.4** and **Figure 2.5**). Tagging was also used to improve the find-ability of message board content and to make it easier for journalists to find emerging local stories by watching tags bubble up over time.

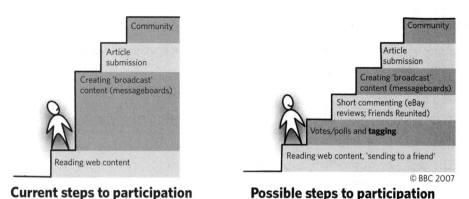

Current steps to participation   **Possible steps to participation**

© BBC 2007

Figure 2.4 In one project, the BBC used tagging to lower barriers to participation.

Figure 2.5 The BBC message board showing what people are talking about in Bristol

Identifying Patterns

Tags give you a wealth of information about people's vocabularies, their opinions, and how they use your resources.

Tagging systems can help you understand these patterns.

- Tagging patterns can tell whether your content has enduring popularity or whether it's a one-hit wonder.

- The tags people use will help you understand whether they find the content useful, interesting, or funny.

- Tags may give you information about how people are using your content.

- Finally, by looking at who is tagging your page, you'll be able to learn more about your users (and the other information they find useful).

Augmenting Existing Classification Efforts

If you already maintain a navigation system for your Web site, or a taxonomy for your intranet, tagging can be a way to augment your existing systems.

Tagging can complement your current classification practices by helping you understand how users describe resources.

Tags contributed by users can be a quick "first pass" at classification, before resources are added to an organizational taxonomy or metadata scheme.

Tags can then be migrated into more formal classification schemes, such as a taxonomy or controlled vocabulary. We'll discuss these approaches in more detail in Chapter 4.

Sparking Innovation

You might not think of tagging as source of innovation, but an interesting pattern consistently emerges in systems that provide both tags and data feeds.

Data feeds are a way to pull information out of your tagging system. When you architect your tagging system to provide a data feed for every single tag, you've created a basic read-write system for your application.

Users can write data through tagging, and they can extract it using a data feed. Interestingly, this has enabled many innovative tagging mash-ups and services. *Geotagging*—using tags to assign latitude and longitude coordinates to resources—began as a simple set of tagging conventions and a system that used data feeds to grab that geographic data and place it on a map (discussed at more length in Chapter 5).

Tagging systems that provide data feeds for their tags often get the benefit of user-generated innovation.

One More Thing: Align Your Efforts

You've already guessed that some of the personal incentives of the people who use tagging systems connect well with the potential business benefits of tagging. You'll get the greatest value by creating your system with your users' motivations in mind.

Here are some suggestions:

- Regardless of your goals for your tagging system, it will succeed only if people actually use it. Your first job is to make it easy for people to contribute.

- If you seek descriptive metadata or are looking at ways to augment your existing classification efforts, you'll want to make sure your tagging system helps people manage their information well.

- If your tagging system is meant to help you understand how people are using your content, social influence can be a negative factor. The visibility of other users' tags may cause some users to simply follow along or even discourage others who have different points of view. You might want to design your system so it minimizes the trails of other users.

- You can help increase participation by encouraging collaboration, play, and self-expression through tags. These behaviors often emerge on their own—as long as the system itself doesn't stifle them.

How you decide to balance return on experience and return on investment will depend on your goals and your users' needs. Should you wonder whether tagging can make a difference to your users, read the sidebar interview with Timo Hannay about tagging in science.

Timo Hannay: The Value of Tagging for Science

Timo Hannay is the director of Web publishing at Nature Publishing Group, which runs the social bookmarking application Connotea.

What kind of information management challenges do scientists face?

We're just really in the early stages of finding out. There's a real explosion of information of all kinds. There's written information, there's data, there's primary experimental data, and then there's data derived through analysis from that. There are all kinds of information that scientists need to be able to get their hands on in order to do their jobs effectively.

So just the volume of information is one thing.

The other sort of really fundamental challenge is that science exists on the frontiers of human knowledge by necessity. If you're not at the frontiers of human knowledge, you're not being a scientist. And the trouble when you're at the frontiers is when you get a new piece of information, you don't know how to classify it. You don't know how it quite fits into the big theme of things. For example, nanotechnology when it began wasn't called *nanotechnology*; it was called something else.

How might tagging influence how scientists find and use information?

It's just unrealistic to expect any individual organization, whether it's the Library of Congress or the Nature Publishing Group or some other organization, to go back and recategorize the archive in light of current understanding and experience.

But it is probably feasible to expect scientists collectively to do that, at least for papers that are particularly interesting or useful. So I think that whole collaborative categorization approach is particularly important in science because the nomenclature inevitably lags the discoveries themselves.

And sometimes nomenclature changes for other reasons. People discover the same gene simultaneously and call it two different things, and suddenly they realize it's the same one and say "Why don't we try to give it one name?" And so the post hoc categorization or tagging of content by using a community-driven approach rather than relying on it being done centrally has some particular potential in science.

Summary

■ Tagging works because it's flexible, extensible, simple, and aggregatable.

■ People are motivated to tag because it helps them manage their information. It also gives information management a social component that lets people share ideas, express themselves, and have fun.

■ Organizations that implement tagging can look for seven benefits. Some of these—such as improved collaboration, increased participation, and enhanced findability—affect the users of the system. Other benefits—such as collecting metadata, supplementing current investments in classification, and identifying how people use resources—are more administrative.

■ You'll get the most value from tagging by figuring out how to align your users' goals (and their return on experience) with your system's goals (and your return on investment).

3 Tagging System Architecture

WHAT YOU'LL LEARN IN THIS CHAPTER:

- The high-level choices you'll make when architecting your tagging system
- The users-resources-tags model in detail
- Architecture of four popular tagging systems
- Five common problems and how to avoid them

The simplicity and flexibility of tagging makes for some complex design decisions. The architecture of your tagging system—the rules that govern the interaction between users, resources, and tags—will have a profound impact on your system's success.

Yahoo's now-defunct Podcasts site provides a useful example. Yahoo Podcasts allowed you to tag podcasts—blog-like audio series shared over the Web. But after you pressed the Submit button, the tags no longer belonged to you. They appeared in the collective pool of tags, but they weren't obviously tethered to your user account. This made it difficult, if not impossible, to find the tags you had used before. Thus, if you tagged NPR's *Science Friday* podcast with "science"... well, there was just no way to find the things you'd tagged as "science" again (see **Figure 3.1**). Your tags disappeared into the ether.

Figure 3.1 The podcast *Science Friday* received many tags, but there was no obvious way for users to find the tags they had used before.

Yahoo Podcasts raises some important questions about how you architect a tagging system. What should be tagged—a podcast series or an individual episode? How do the resources (in this case podcasts) get into the system? Should tagging be limited to contributors, or should listeners be able to tag as well? What do you do when the people tagging are different from the people creating and contributing resources?

Welcome to the occasionally knotty world of tag system design. In this chapter we're going to discuss the architecture of your tagging system in detail. We'll start by digging into the model of tagging systems introduced in Chapter 1 and looking at the more abstract design choices you'll have to make. We'll look at the architecture of four popular tagging systems. Finally, we'll examine some of the common pitfalls that come with designing tagging systems.

Users, Resources, and Tags: Exploring Our Three-Part Model of Tagging

In Chapter 1 you were introduced to a three-part model of tagging where users add tags to resources in a system (see **Figure 3.2**). Before you start designing your interface or planning social navigation features, you'll want to think about the relationships and rules between users, resources, and tags in your tagging system.

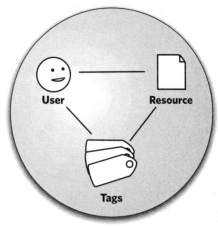

Tagging System

Figure 3.2 The architecture of your tagging system involves defining the rules and relationships between users, resources, and tags.

In other words, you'll want to think about the architecture of your tagging system. In this context, *architecture* simply means the abstract design decisions involved in creating a tagging system. The functionality and feel of a tagging application is determined to a significant extent by these architectural considerations.

We're going to break down all three parts of the model—users, resources, and tags—and talk about the choices involved for each one. Some of these choices will involve trade-offs, such as introducing social components that influence the kinds of tags people contribute. The goal of this chapter is for you to understand those trade-offs so you can make the best design decisions for your tagging system.

Part 1: Users

It's no stretch to say that users are the essential, active ingredient of any tagging system. When you're planning your tagging system, you should think about how your users become part of the system, what happens to the resources they contribute, and whether they can connect with other users.

IDENTITY: WHO ARE THEY?

The first and arguably the most important question to ask is "who are my users?"

Even though tagging is becoming mainstream, not everyone understands how to use it or what it's for. The Pew Internet & American Life Project found that as much as 7 percent of U.S. Internet users were tagging daily. But these people were more like typical early adopters than a soccer mom in suburban Michigan or a retired school bus driver in Mississippi.

You will probably already know who your users are in a general way. If you're running an intranet, your users are probably the staff of your organization. If you operate an e-commerce site, they're likely your customers.

If you're concerned about whether they will grok tagging, try using one of these techniques:

- **Surveys**. Send out a questionnaire to gather data about your users. In addition to asking for demographic information, you could also ask whether they've ever organized content online, used another tagging system, or played with a social networking site.

- **Interviews**. Sit down with your users face to face and ask them about their information sharing habits. You could even have them test-drive one of the more popular tagging sites.

- **Fieldwork**. Observe users going about their day-to-day business, and ask yourself how your tagging system helps them. Does it alleviate a pain point? Does it help them solve a problem? Does it make an existing task easier?

The more effort you spend understanding your users, the more likely you'll be to design a system that fits their needs.

MEMBERSHIP: HOW DO THEY GET INTO THE SYSTEM?

Now that you know who your users are, you'll have to consider how they get to be members of the system.

As the old ad slogan goes, membership has its privileges. In the case of tagging systems, membership might include the ability to add resources, to create tags, and to watch other people's tags and resources.

Let's look at three kinds of membership:

- **Public sign-up**. People join the system by signing up for it. Most of the consumer tagging systems we describe in this book follow this model.

- **Invitation only**. New members are invited by existing members. This is often used when applications are being tested and aren't yet ready for public release.

- **External criteria**. Membership is determined by factors outside the scope of your system. For example, if your organization runs an internal social bookmarking application, users might become members simply by being on staff.

I once designed a tagging system for a government client where anyone on staff in the department could add and edit tags. People from other departments could view tags but not edit them. And, unfortunately, I couldn't participate at all because I was a contractor.

What happens when you don't explicitly determine membership? You might end up with something like Yahoo Podcasts where there are no apparent relationships between users and tags and you can't even find the tags you've submitted.

TURNOVER: WHAT HAPPENS TO THEM?

Every company experiences turnover—some people leave to take on new jobs, while others join to fill the vacancies. This happens with users in tagging systems too, and it will have implications for your system.

Turnover means the rate that users join and leave. For most consumer Web sites, inactive users can pick up where they left off months or years after they create their account.

For internal tagging applications, you may have to decide what to do when employees leave an organization. You might be tempted to mothball their accounts, and their tags with them, so that they're no longer visible to other users. After all, if they're no longer contributing members of the organization, why should you keep their bookmarks, photos, and tags around?

One clear and sensible reason is that the tags supplied by people long gone may be valuable trails for newcomers. Indeed, retaining their resources and tags can be a way of minimizing the cost of lost knowledge when an employee walks out the door.

If you can, keep the accounts of departed users available but inactive.

ACTIVITY: HOW ENTHUSIASTIC ARE THEY?

Activity means the frequency with which users post resources and tags. A highly active user base is desirable but not always possible.

User activity is a good estimate for the volume and dynamism of your resources and tags. Many of your interface decisions, especially those around social navigation, will be driven by user activity. For example, a highly active user base might want to see tagging trends rather than the absolute popularity of tags. For a less active user base, trends might not change enough to be interesting.

Of course, you can't really know how active your users will be until they're engaged with your system. But there are some ways you can estimate activity:

- Start with a pilot or beta, and watch how people use the system.

- Consider how receptive your users have been to other technologies. If they've been speedy adopters of similar systems—such as blogs and wikis—there's a good chance they'll pick up tags quickly.

- Look at users' pain points around sharing and finding information. If your tagging system resolves that pain, you'll likely see greater interest and activity.

One interesting property of tagging systems is that user activity seems to generate the same kind of pattern—known as a *power law*—regardless of the kind of content or tags people use. The power law is discussed later in this chapter.

COMMUNITY: HOW DO THEY ENGAGE WITH OTHER USERS?

The social hum that happens in tagging systems can be a powerful way of motivating participation. Though there are cases where it may be unneeded, most tagging systems thrive when they include a social component.

Let's consider three types of connections between users (see **Figure 3.3**):

- *Followers* are simple one-way connections between users. Any user can follow any other user. Del.icio.us uses a followers model, where connections can be mutual but don't have to be.

- *Contacts* are reciprocal connections between users. A user can ask another user to be a contact, and if that user agrees, a two-way connection is made between them. Facebook uses a contacts system.

- *Groups* are collections of users who join together to share resources about a particular topic. A user may need permission from an administrator to join a group. Ma.gnolia's groups, for example, add another layer of organization to its bookmarks. Ma.gnolia also uses contacts.

Figure 3.3 Three kinds of user-to-user relationships: (1) groups in Ma.gnolia, (2) contacts in Facebook, and (3) followers in Del.icio.us.

These connections are the foundation of social navigation—finding information by following the streams of other people.

But even if you don't build navigation options around user-to-user connections, expos-ing user actions in your tagging system can still have value. Passive users, or *lurkers*, can watch how other people post and tag resources and then follow along. Letting active users function as role models creates a positive form of social proof.

Part 2: Resources

Up to this point we've talked about people contributing and tagging resources such as Web pages or photos. But as you might've guessed, there's a bit more to it than that. You do not always contribute the resources you tag, and sometimes the thing you think you are tagging is not what you are actually tagging.

CONTRIBUTIONS: HOW DOES IT GET INTO THE SYSTEM?

Let's look at two ways resources can enter your tagging system:

- A system can have *user-contributed resources*, where bookmarks, photos, and videos are added by users on an ongoing basis. Flickr, Del.icio.us, YouTube, SlideShare, and most other collecting and sharing Web sites have user-contributed resources.

- In the case of *system resources*, the resources are part of an existing catalog or database. They may be added through another process that has nothing to do with tagging. In any case, these resources aren't contributed or owned by any user. Amazon's product catalog is a good example of system resources.

These models aren't mutually exclusive. LibraryThing has a vast amount of data on published books from library and ISBN records. However, if you have a book that isn't in one of LibraryThing's 82-source databases, you can still add it to your library and tag it. Thus, LibraryThing mixes user-contributed resources and system resources.

ORIGINAL OR POINTER: WHAT EXACTLY IS BEING TAGGED?

The resource is the document, link, photo, or video that people tag. But understanding what *exactly* is being tagged is not as simple as it seems.

In some cases we tag the *original* resource—it might be the actual document, photo, or video, or it might be an authoritative database record for that resource. In any case, even if multiple people are tagging it, all the tags are applied to that one resource.

In social bookmarking systems people are tagging a bookmark, or a URL. However, their tags aren't attached to the actual Web page they've bookmarked but to a record in a database that contains the URL. We'll call this a *pointer*—a record that stands for the resource being tagged. The social bookmarking example is apropos since a pointer is kind of like a bookmark.

The key distinction between an original resource and a pointer is that there is just one original, and there can be as many pointers as there are people tagging that resource. See **Figure 3.4**.

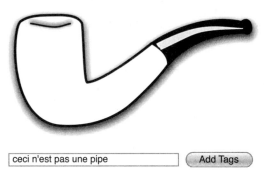

ceci n'est pas une pipe   Add Tags

Figure 3.4 Just like Magritte's famous painting invites us to consider the differences between an object and its image, tagging systems sometimes reveal that the connection between metadata (tags) and data (resources) isn't as clear as we think.

Does this seem abstract and complicated? It is. But it's also one of the most fundamental distinctions within tagging systems. Systems that use pointers are collaborative—many people can tag the same resource with their own unique tags. Systems that use originals are not collaborative at the resource level, although you can still aggregate tags across users. (Technically, there are very few cases where you actually tag the resource directly. This is covered in the section "Truth: Where Are the Tags?" later in this chapter.)

PRIVACY: WHO CAN SEE IT?

We'll talk a lot about the value of social tagging in this book. But there are cases where your users may want, or demand, the ability to keep their resources private.

One possible concern is that using a public social bookmarking system for work-related research would turn your bookmarks stream into a source of competitive intelligence. There are also things we research on the Web that we might like to tag and keep track of but that we just don't want other people seeing. One commenter on the Del.icio.us blog talks about the privacy needed for his research on Chlamydia home-testing kits. Enough said!

We can consider four kinds of privacy:

- **Everything is public**. Del.icio.us began as a public system where every link was available to every other user. It added private bookmarks later. Its openness helped establish social hum, but it also kept some users away.

- **Configurable, but public by default**. You might allow the privacy settings to be configurable based on the community features you implement. By making the default settings public, you encourage people to share their resources and tags (see **Figure 3.5**).

- **Configurable, but private by default**. You could also make the default settings private, which may make users feel more secure but discourages sharing.

- **Everything is private**. Finally, all resources and tags can be private with no option to share.

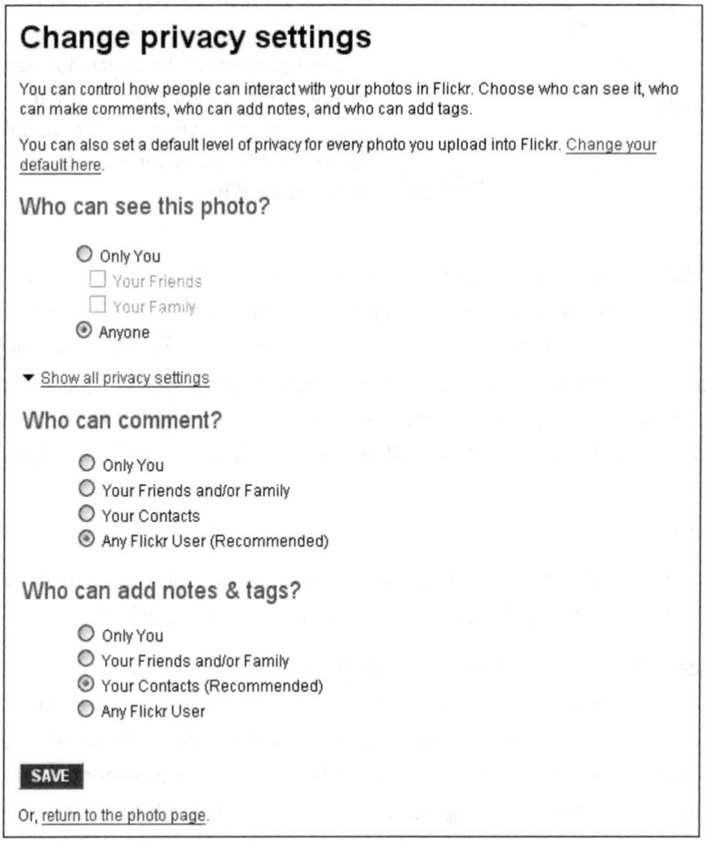

Figure 3.5 Flickr allows you to set the permissions for visibility, comments, and tags separately.

As you can probably tell, the sociability of your tagging system depends greatly on your default privacy settings.

RESTRICTIONS: WHAT ISN'T ALLOWED?

Another issue to consider is whether there are any restrictions or limitations on the resources.

A system could limit resources by the following:

- **File type**. Flickr is limited to image files, Del.icio.us to links.

- **Object**. In LibraryThing, people tag books in their library.

- **Genre**. Yahoo Podcasts was limited to a particular genre of audio.

- **Origin**. Your system might support tagging documents only on an internal Web site, for example.

In many cases, these restrictions will be obvious to users (it's not likely that someone would join a photo-sharing site and expect to share bookmarks).

DYNAMISM: HOW FAST DOES THE SYSTEM MOVE?

Finally, the number of resources in your system and the rate at which they change will influence the way people use the system.

If resources are contributed by users, you can (probably) expect a continual stream of additions. How fast that stream moves depends on how active your users are.

If your resources are already part of the system, or if they enter through another process (we called this the *system resources* model earlier), then the size and rate of change in the collection might not correlate to user activity.

The upside of user-contributed resources is that resources can be submitted and tagged at the same time. In a case where resources already exist in the system, users may not feel as strong a motivation to tag.

Anticipating how dynamic your resource collection will be will help you do the following:

- Design navigation and visualization tools. Highly dynamic systems can be a blur of activity, which means your interface should highlight relevant trends rather than try to show everything that's happening.

- Set your expectations about the kind and quality of tags you'll get. In fast-moving systems, where people add dozens of resources a day, tags may be nothing more than a few quick ideas jotted down. In systems with a more languid pace, tags may be more thoughtful.

Going back to the stream metaphor we used in Chapter 1, the speed of your stream will influence more concrete design decisions such as navigation.

Part 3: Tags

You already know what tags are: the keywords attached to resources by users. As we've already discussed, the kinds of tags you'll get are strongly influenced by the decisions you make around users and resources.

You'll want to recognize early on how decisions about tagging permissions, privacy, and community can affect the kind of tags people contribute. The choices you make should be informed by the user and business goals we discussed in Chapter 2. The right decisions will be the ones that help you achieve your goals, but along the way you might have to make trade-offs between some features.

PERMISSIONS: WHO CAN TAG WHAT?

In many arenas of life, we give other people permission to do something for us. You give your accountant permission to file your taxes. Or you might give your kids permission to use your credit card.

Some tagging systems let you give other users permission to tag your resources. More generally, we can think of permissions as the system's rules for determining the following:

- Who can create, edit and delete tags
- The resources for which they can create, edit, and delete tags

Most tagging systems with user-contributed resources have a simple and straightforward way of determining permissions. The people who contribute resources get to tag them and can add, edit, or remove the tags later if they want.

In some cases, these permissions can be extended to other users in the system. In Flickr, for example, you can give your contacts and friends permission to tag your photos (they can also delete the tags they add). Figure 3.5 (see page 48) shows Flickr's default setting for tagging permissions.

When you're dealing with system resources, the first permissions-related issue you'll have to consider is whether to allow tagging at all. After that you may want to limit tagging to just a subset of your collection. The choices you make here will have to be based on the specifics of your tagging system.

One common faux pas when dealing with system resources is to leave tags disconnected from a user's identity. On the surface this might seem valuable, since you'll collect a lot more metadata if people can tag resources without signing up, logging in, or performing some other action that confirms their identity.

But you also lose much of the value of tagging, and you create a disincentive for your users. When people can't easily re-find resources—because there's no way to tell one user's tags from another—they quickly lose some of their motivation to tag. And when it comes to editing tags, you might have to let everyone edit (or delete) every tag. Yahoo Podcasts went the other direction: it gave people the right to assign tags, but no one could change them or delete them.

I won't say that this kind of tagging is wrong, but it's certainly less than ideal. If you go this route, be prepared for a free-for-all.

TRUTH: WHERE ARE THE TAGS?

Flickr keeps multiple copies of every photo you post. None of them actually contains the tags you add on the photo page. The tags are applied to a database record that represents your photo. (Microsoft's Photo Gallery application, discussed later in the book, stores your tags in the photo itself.)

That brings us to the issue of truth. In this context, *truth* refers to the canonical place where metadata is stored. For our purposes, there are two kinds of truth:

- *The truth is in the file* means that the tags are stored in the file (or resource) itself. They're portable; they go wherever the file goes.

- *The truth is in the database* means that the tags are stored outside the resource, most often in a database. While the tags aren't as easily portable, they can follow the resource if it moves. For social bookmarking applications that don't have any access to the actual bookmarked page, database truth is the only option.

This might seem like an esoteric subject, but it has some practical implications. If you're implementing a social bookmarking system on your intranet, the tags will probably be added to a database rather than the documents themselves. For the tags to improve search results, you'll have to make sure your search engine indexes the tags in the database as well as the documents.

Portability of tags is another issue to keep in mind. In a social bookmarking system, when a bookmarked site changes location, its tags do not move with it. If you redesign your Web site and change your URLs, you'll break the connection between people's tags and bookmarks.

CONTROL: SHOULD YOU CENSOR TAGS?

You might also want to think about whether there should be restrictions on using certain words as tags. Amazon, for example, blocks common expletives from being used as tags. Depending on your users and their attitudes, this could be a form of sensible censorship.

Many other tagging systems don't block expletives and have no apparent problems. If you're not sure what to do, try these solutions:

- Monitor your system to see how people use potentially objectionable tags. You'll want to understand whether these tags are a form of abuse or whether they're accurate descriptions of the resource.

- Ask your users to flag inappropriate tags and resources. This kind of social policing can help foster a sense of community as well as reduce the incidence of offensive material.

You have to be wary about exercising too much control. Your users might use tags that express an opinion you don't like but isn't otherwise objectionable. If users feel stifled or unreasonably censored, they may abandon your system.

(The "Bad Actors: Curbing Antisocial Behavior" section later in this chapter has some suggestions for dealing with troublesome users.)

PATTERNS: UNDERSTANDING THE POWER LAW

One pattern that consistently emerges in tagging systems is the power law. A *power law* is a distribution characterized by a few elements occurring with a high frequency and most with a low frequency.

Figure 3.6 shows a typical power-law curve. This curve turns up all over the Web: a few Web sites attract the most links, a few pages on your site get most of your traffic, and most of your traffic comes from a few sources.

You can find the power-law pattern in other fields as well. Economist Vilfredo Pareto noticed that 80 percent of wealth was held by 20 percent of the population. Alfred Lotka found that a few authors write most scientific articles, while many authors write just one. George Zipf discovered that word frequencies follow the same trend—a few words, such as *the,* are used most often, while others are much rarer. In fact, the power law is often called Zipf's law, and it appears just about everywhere, including mathematics, physics, economics, and bibliometrics, to name just a few disciplines.

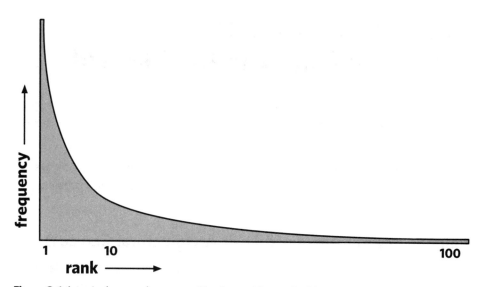

Figure 3.6 A typical power-law curve. The item with a rank of 1 occurs many times more often than the item with rank 10 (similarly with items 10 and 100).

It's no surprise then that it occurs in tagging systems as well. One study—"Complex Dynamics of Collaborative Tagging" by Harry Halpin, Valentin Robu, and Hana Shepherd—analyzed 500 popular bookmarks from Del.icio.us and found that a power-law curve consistently emerged for each resource. There was also very little difference between the shapes of the curves across different sites.

This is an important finding: regardless of the content of the site or the tags people used, *the distribution of tags followed the same pattern*. (For less popular sites, the power-law curve was still evident, but there was more variation in its shape.)

Why does the power law turn up so consistently? The authors developed a model based on *preferential attachment*, the idea that once a tag has been used, there's a greater probability it will be used again. Social proof, suggestion interfaces, and other factors could also contribute to this effect.

The prevalence of the power law will influence many of the design choices in your tagging system. For example, creating a tag cloud requires compensating for the massive popularity of a few tags (covered in Chapter 5).

Tagging in Practice: Examples from the Real World

We've now examined some of the major architectural considerations for your tagging system. These issues are important on their own, but what's more important is how they work together as a whole.

In the following sections, we'll look at the architecture of four different tagging systems and discuss their similarity and differences. We'll also consider five problems that recur in tagging systems.

Four Tagging Systems (and Their Architectural Choices)

Tagging is often seen as a homogeneous feature—many people think one implementation is the same as another. But as we just discussed, designing a tagging system involves several important decisions.

Let's look at how four different systems handle those decisions. **Table 3.1** shows the choices made by Del.icio.us, Flickr, Amazon, and Microsoft's photo management application Photo Gallery in the major categories we've just discussed. (Categories such as the system's users, turnover, and activity aren't addressed in this table since it's difficult to assess those without inside information about the system.)

Table 3.1 Architectural Differences Between Four Tagging Systems

	Del.icio.us	**Flickr**	**Amazon**	**Photo Gallery**
Users				
Membership	Public sign-up	Public sign-up	Public sign-up	Private
Community	Followers	Groups	Contacts	N/A
Resources				
Contributions	User contributed	User contributed	System resources	User contributed
Original/Pointer	Pointer	Original	Pointer	Original
Privacy	Configurable Public default	Configurable Public default	Configurable Public default	Private
Restrictions	URLs only	Images only	Catalog items only	Images only

table 3.1 continued

	Del.icio.us	**Flickr**	**Amazon**	**Photo Gallery**
Tags				
Permissions	None	Configurable	N/A	N/A
Truth	Database	Database	Database	File
Control	None	None	Yes	None

It's worth pausing here to emphasize the significance of tagging a pointer versus tagging the original resource.

COLLABORATIVE TAGGING

Despite their many differences, Del.icio.us and Amazon both have users tagging a pointer. This means that each user has his or her own unique set of tags for that resource, and those tags can be aggregated to create a consensus view of each resource. We'll call this a *collaborative tagging* model.

SIMPLE TAGGING

Flickr and Photo Gallery use what we'll call *simple tagging* systems. Because they allow tagging of the original resource only, there is no aggregate view of tags for resources.

These distinctions are important from an architectural point of view. In Chapter 7 we'll look at the technical design of both simple and collaborative tagging systems.

Five Common Tagging Pitfalls (and Their Solutions)

Most tagging systems—and most social software systems—face a few common obstacles when they start out. These problems usually involve getting people interested in the system, making sense of the data people create, and reducing the impact of antisocial users.

THE COLD-START PROBLEM: BOOSTING INTEREST AND ACTIVITY

Here's a familiar situation faced by many social software systems: you launch the system on Monday and expect it to be abuzz with activity by Wednesday. Things look promising on Friday when a few people try it. But next week, it's dead.

This is the *cold-start* problem. The name suggests it's like trying to start your car on a cold winter's morning, but a better analogy would be throwing a party. People often want to know who's going to be at a party before they're sure whether they want to go. That presents you with a catch-22: it's hard to get people to come to your party unless there are people already going.

The same thing applies to social software systems: people are more likely to use a tagging system if they see other people are already using it. The challenge, then, is getting those first active users.

There are several possible solutions:

- Start with a pilot project or a beta. So when you open up the system to new users, they'll see the activity of your pilot participants.

- Promote your product to the mavens and connectors in your organization. From Malcolm Gladwell's book *The Tipping Point,* mavens are respected experts, and connectors are people with large social networks. Together they can help you create positive buzz for your service.

- Create in-system incentives for tagging. Prominently featuring the names of the most active contributors, for example, is one way to encourage participation. Leaderboards, or rankings, for the most active taggers can encourage competition between users (with the side benefit of more tags).

- Use out-of-system incentives such as promotions or contests to encourage participation.

- If nothing else works, you might consider paying people to tag. Or you could use a service such as Amazon's Mechanical Turk (http://mturk.com) to distribute tagging to online workers. You should understand, though, that the kind and quality of the tags will be different from those added by real users. And your real users may notice the difference. I can suggest this only as a last resort.

MESSY METADATA: A TANGLE OF TAGS

Throughout this book we've extolled the virtues of tagging, especially the flexibility and extensibility it provides. But these virtues come with a price: messiness.

Messy is a pseudo-technical term that describes the following:

- Tags with obvious syntactic problems

- Multiple versions of the same tag with only minor variations in spelling and punctuation

- No apparent patterns in the tag set

Messiness is a potential problem for you as the designer of the tagging system. Messiness can make it harder to extract quality metadata from tags or design social navigation systems.

There are a few ways you can clean up your tags:

- Change the interface so that the tags are more regular. Tag suggestions are one way to reduce the mess.

- Encourage your users to follow conventions—such as using the singular form of the tag rather than the plural.

- Create relationships, like synonyms, between the tags once they're in the system. Be aware, however, that this is a task that usually requires a human touch.

- Use an algorithm to look for patterns in the tags, such as Flickr's clustering or Del.icio.us's co-occurrence algorithm.

The first two solutions actually reduce the mess by encouraging less variation in the tag set. The other ones are just clever ways of hiding it. (And all of these ideas are discussed in upcoming chapters.)

We should also recognize that the term *messy* is a value judgment. Messy compared to what? Tags may be messy when they're held up to rigid corporate taxonomies, perfectly harmonized brand messages composed by marketing departments, or the orderly catalogs maintained by libraries. But for any individual user, their own tags may be perfectly ordered.

There is no rule that says tags have to take on a certain form, obey certain rules, or converge to some predetermined limits. You can influence the tags you get, but ultimately tagging lets users choose the terms that are relevant to them. This means that their tags won't always match your purposes. But you'll almost certainly be surprised by the way they use tags.

VOCAL MINORITY: WHEN USERS USURP YOUR SYSTEM

In social tagging systems, it's easy for a small group of active taggers to dominate the system.

Of course, active taggers can be an incredible asset to your system. At the same time, because of the way tagging systems bubble up popular tags, their tags can dominate a system even when their interests don't reflect those of other users.

Let's say a few people use your tagging system to obsessively document the activities of Paris Hilton, Lindsay Lohan, and other celebrities. Their tags quickly become the most popular tags, which suggests that everyone who uses your system is interested in Hollywood gossip.

You can see evidence of this in Ma.gnolia's Apple group, where many of the top tags have been added by one user. **Figure 3.7** shows how one unusual and highly popular tag, "43," was added by just one person.

Figure 3.7 The most popular tag, "43," in Ma.gnolia's Apple group was added by one user.

The solution to this problem, which we'll cover in more detail in Chapter 5, is to adjust your popularity algorithms so that they're sensitive to user activity.

BAD ACTORS: CURBING ANTISOCIAL BEHAVIOR

Another common problem is what LibraryThing's Tim Spalding calls *bad actors*, or people who try to influence the system for their own gain.

The most common bad actors are spammers, the lowlifes who fill up your inbox with offers of herbal supplements and performance-enhancing pharmaceuticals.

Spam is a problem all over the Web, and it's no surprise that it has found its way into tagging. Yahoo's MyWeb 2.0, a social bookmarking service where tags can help users improve their search results, has been afflicted with mortgage spam in the past (see **Figure 3.8**).

Figure 3.8 Real estate-related spam turns up in the tag cloud on Yahoo's MyWeb 2.0.

Because spammers often use scripts to submit posts, fighting spam resembles an arms race. Your highly effective spam-blocking technique may be useless once the spammer figures out how to route around it.

But we can't limit our discussion to spammers. Anyone who uses your system in an antisocial way—such as someone engaging in hate speech or posting inappropriate material like pornography—can be a bad actor.

Here are some suggestions to fight bad actors in your tagging system:

- To prevent automated submissions, try using a test that separates humans from bots. A CAPTCHA (Completely Automated Public Turing Test for Telling Computers and Humans Apart) is one technique (see **Figure 3.9**). These tests don't always work, but they're an effective way of thwarting simple spammers.

■ Give users an option to ignore or block other users. While this doesn't prevent spam from entering the system, it minimizes its impact.

■ Enlist your users to help identify and flag bad actors or inappropriate resources. Your users have as much motivation to keep bad actors out of the system as you do.

Figure 3.9 SlideShare users help identify and flag inappropriate content.

TIME IS MONEY: MANAGING LIMITED RESOURCES

One great thing about tagging systems is that users do most of the work—adding and tagging resources according to their own interests and motivations.

But depending on your goals, your tagging system might still require administration and maintenance—in other words, time and money beyond your initial investment in developing it.

Here are some ways to stretch your budget and get more value out of your tagging system:

■ Make it easy to get the data you'll need to manage the system. Consider designing a dashboard that shows you recent activity and relevant trends for your users, resources, and tags (see **Figure 3.10**).

■ You should also consider having your users perform some administrative tasks— such as managing tags and flagging outdated resources. LibraryThing lets its users combine tags (which effectively makes two tags synonyms). This helps reduce the number of distinct tags in LibraryThing and makes the overall tag collection more useful—and it's done entirely by users.

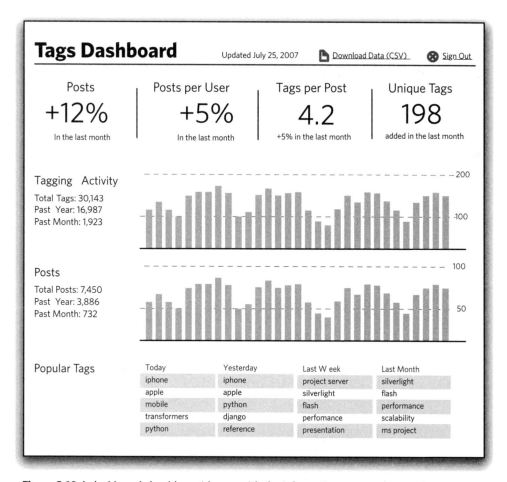

Figure 3.10 A dashboard should provide you with the information you need to monitor, manage, and report on your tagging system.

Summary

- The architecture of your tagging system requires you to set rules about your users (who they are and how they join the system), your resources (how they're added to the system), and tags (who can tag which resources).

- You'll need to consider how users become part of the system and how they interact with other users.

■ For your resources, you'll have to think about how they get into the system, who can view or tag them, and whether to limit them to certain file types or formats.

■ Although they're similar in some superficial ways, popular tagging sites such as Del.icio.us, Flickr, Amazon, and Photo Gallery have architected their tagging systems differently. Del.icio.us and Amazon are examples of collaborative tagging, while Flickr and Photo Gallery employ what we'll call *simple tagging*.

■ The cold-start problem, messy metadata, vocal minorities, and bad actors are common problems with most tagging systems (and most social software systems as well).

4 Tags, Metadata, and Classification Systems

WHAT YOU'LL LEARN IN THIS CHAPTER:

- How tags function as metadata

- How to mix tags with controlled vocabularies, taxonomies, and facets

- Four features of folksonomies

- Different philosophies on tags as part of a metadata ecosystem

You'll be relieved to know that if you're fatally bitten by a Gila monster while line dancing at a Six Flags, the World Health Organization's International Classification of Diseases (ICD) has a code reserved for just such an event. It's X20.81, and it breaks down like this:

- External causes of morbidity and mortality (V01–Y98)

- Accidents (V01–X59)

- Contact with venomous animals or plants (X20–29)

- Contact with venomous snakes and lizards (X20)

- Other specified place (8, which includes amusement parks)

- While engaged in leisure activity (1, which includes dancing)

If that seems like an unlikely occurrence (no one actually line dances anymore, right?), the ICD also includes codes for more common events. If you've ever worked in an office, you've probably experienced F15.5, which covers hallucination due to overcaffeination.

These are amusing examples, but the ICD is serious business. More than 100 countries use the ICD to classify illnesses and deaths and to calculate important statistics about the health of their population. It's one of the most widely used classification systems in the world. You can find all kinds of bizarre and macabre disease codes within the ICD, simply because it has to include all known causes of death, illness, and injury.

Classification systems aim to help make information more findable and usable by removing some of the ambiguity of language. Sometimes classification systems exist to establish an order where none existed before or to support the collection of knowledge. Like the ICD, many classification systems aim to be comprehensive within their domain. But as our world changes, these systems inevitably fall behind. The first paper on AIDS was published in 1983, but it took three years for the disease to enter the ICD (and that was considered relatively speedy).

Note

For more on the International Classification of Diseases, visit http://www.who. int/classifications/icd/en/.

This chapter will look at how tags can augment classification systems to make them more flexible and to reflect the views of their users. We'll consider how tags can work with controlled vocabularies, taxonomies, and faceted classification. And we'll explore *folksonomies*—user-generated classification systems based on tags—and the situations where they work well. But first we'll look at tags as a form of metadata.

Metadata for the Masses

Tagging is an approach to collecting metadata, and metadata is a big topic. Every electronic transaction we perform—from buying a Slurpee to searching the Web—relies on some form of metadata. People spend their lives designing schemas and debating the philosophical nuances of data, meta and otherwise.

But we don't need to get bogged down in the metaphysics of metadata. A brief tour of the popular perspectives on metadata will help you understand what makes tagging different from other approaches.

Three Kinds of Metadata: Descriptive, Administrative, and Structural

In Chapter 1 we defined metadata as "data about data," but the standard approach to metadata might be better described as "documentation for your data." Like other kinds of documentation, metadata helps you understand and use your data.

Metadata is typically used for one of these purposes:

- It helps you (or others) find data you want.

- It's helps you manage your data (your personal data or data belonging to your organization).

- It lets you relate your data to other data you own (as well as other data out there in the world).

In the world of digital libraries, the metadata that performs these functions is divided into three categories: descriptive, administrative, and structural.

DESCRIPTIVE METADATA

Descriptive metadata provides details about the resource. For digital documents, it can include a title, an abstract, the name of the author or authors, and subject headings.

In some cases, certain kinds of information require specialized description metadata. A metadata record for a sculpture, for example, might include the materials used and when it was made. A painting could include measurements, materials, and the subject of the painting. If it's a landscape painting, the subject might be a physical location.

ADMINISTRATIVE METADATA

Administrative metadata is used to manage a collection of resources. The collection could be physical objects such as the books owned by a library or digital files such as the pages on a Web site.

Examples of administrative metadata include the date a resource was acquired, the person who owns the rights to the resource, and the contact information for someone responsible for the resource. Administrative metadata can also include information about the tools used to create the resource. Organizations that keep digital resources often need information on the computers, files, and formats used to create them so they can be accessed in the future.

Web site content management systems often make good use of administrative metadata to track who authored a Web page and when it needs to be revised.

STRUCTURAL METADATA

Structural metadata is used to associate the resource with other resources. Structural metadata might include page or volume numbers for books. Companies that convert books to digital text use structural metadata to associate the electronic words with their original pages (helpful when optical character recognition doesn't recognize as well as it should). For digital resources, structural metadata can mean a map of how the individual files that make up a resource relate to each other.

One important difference between these three kinds of metadata is their level of precision. Some metadata, often the administrative and structural kind, can be quite exact and unambiguous. Dates, author names, and page and volume numbers all have precise values.

Descriptive metadata, on the other hand, can often be subjective. For example, selecting the subject headings that best fit a sculpture could require both domain knowledge and personal interpretation.

Tags as Metadata

Tags are certainly metadata, but they aren't so easily separated into categories like descriptive, administrative, and structural. As we know from Chapter 2, people tag for different reasons, and tagging systems themselves can be designed with different purposes in mind.

In most cases, however, tags perform one of seven functions as metadata. **Table 4.1** shows these seven tag types along with examples. These seven categories were pulled from two important papers: "Structure of Collaborative Tagging Systems" by Scott Golder and Bernardo Huberman, and "Position Paper, Tagging, Taxonomy, Flickr, Article, WWW2006, ToRead" by Cameron Marlow, Mor Naaman, danah boyd, and Marc Davis.

These seven tag types are reasonably complete but by no means exhaustive. A deep analysis of tags would probably reveal niche categories of tags that perform highly specialized functions for certain users. And sometimes tags can be completely idiosyncratic—their meaning and purpose is known only to their creator.

Table 4.1 Seven Kinds of Tags

Tag Type	Examples
Descriptive	css, webdesign, ajax, Minnesota, drama, gardening, zen, microfinance, music, halo3, networks, sushi, hibiscus
Resource	blog, book, video, photo
Ownership/Source	nytimes, genesmith (author), newriders
Opinion	cool, funny,*****, lame, beautiful, crap, defective by design
Self-reference	mystuff, mine, me
Task Organizing	toread, todo, work
Play and Performance	squaredcircle, seenlive, aka vogon poetry

The first four tag types are primarily descriptive in nature and are similar to the kinds of descriptive metadata often stored by libraries. Traditional metadata schemes often don't have a place for users' opinions, but most librarians and information architects *are* interested in what people think is popular, cool, lame, and funny. With tags, however, some, none, or all these tag types might be used when tagging a resource.

A person's choice of tags may depend on why a person is tagging in the first place. Marlow et al. suggest that people's motivations for tagging will determine the kinds of tags they use. People whose primary goal is personal information management might stick to descriptive and task-related tags. Others who enjoy the social aspects of tagging will likely branch out into opinion and performance tagging. (For an explanation of the tag "aka vogon poetry" and more about opinion and performance tags, Google Alla Zollers's paper "Emerging Motivations for Tagging: Expression, Performance, and Activism.")

So, that's metadata. Next we'll look at a broader question: how do you organize metadata into structures that help people find and use information?

Taxonomies and Controlled Vocabularies

Taxonomies and controlled vocabularies are two kinds of classification systems that define relationships between terms. These relationships can be semantic—like establishing that "math" and "arithmetic" are synonyms. They can also be conceptual—like the relationship between philosophy and epistemology, a branch of philosophy that's concerned with the nature of knowledge. They can even disambiguate terms with multiple meanings like "bank" (a financial institution and the land beside a river).

Taxonomies and controlled vocabularies help us understand and navigate concepts by making language less ambiguous, by connecting concepts, and by capturing the relationship between objects observed in the real world. Just like metadata, some of these relationships can be exact (like the relationship between a book and its subject categories), while others are more subjective (for example, placing Stephen King's novels in the Classics section).

Some people believe that tagging is a radical departure from these kinds of classification systems. And it is, in that it involves the contributions of users and allows people to put a resource in multiple categories. But tagging can also complement traditional classification systems, and we'll look at several examples of that in the following sections.

Controlled Vocabularies

Here's an easy question: what generic word do you use to describe a carbonated beverage?

If you're from the northern United States or Canada, chances are that you'll say "pop." If you're from the Southwest or Northeast U.S., you'll probably say "soda." If you're from the Southern U.S., particularly the Gulf States, the odds are that your generic name for a soft drink is "coke."

Note

Alan McConchie asked this very question on his Web site http://popvssoda.com.

All of these words refer to the same concept; for any discussion related to beverages, they are essentially synonyms. (*Soda* can also refer to chemicals containing sodium, and sodium bicarbonate is sometimes used to make soda water.)

A controlled vocabulary is a system for managing the meaning of words. It removes some of the ambiguity of language and ensures that people who use "pop," "soda," or "coke" can find the carbonated beverage they're after. In generic terms, controlled vocabularies help with recall so you don't have to look for one thing using multiple terms.

The two most common kinds of controlled vocabularies are *synonym rings* and *authority files*.

SYNONYM RINGS

A synonym ring gives two or more words an equivalent meaning. Synonyms can be useful for smoothing out the differences between acronyms and their fully expanded names or for handling equivalence in regional variations. **Figure 4.1** shows how simple synonym rings work.

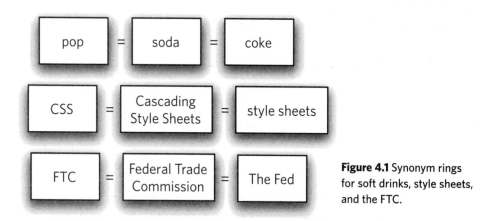

Figure 4.1 Synonym rings for soft drinks, style sheets, and the FTC.

One particularly good use of synonym rings is to tune a search engine to recognize equivalent terms (like "FTC" and "Federal Trade Commission") and return results for all them.

AUTHORITY FILES

An authority file is similar to a synonym ring, but one of the words is identified as a preferred term. The authoritative term is displayed to users, while the other terms may be used to provide pointers to the authoritative term (for example, "for information about 'soda,' see our page on 'pop'").

Authority files are helpful for mapping popular terms, nicknames, variations, and abbreviations to one official term. For example, "pop" and "soda" can be alternate terms for "soft drink." Hip-hop music, where recording artists often change their names, is one unlikely source of many informal authority files (see **Figure 4.2**).

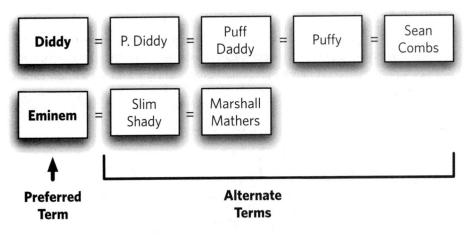

Figure 4.2 Hip-hop authority files for Diddy and Eminem.

What's In a Word?

We all remember synonyms and homonyms from grade school. Let's take a moment to introduce some of the more esoteric terms for describing lexical relationships.

- *Homographs* are words with the same spelling but distinct meanings. For example, a ship has a bow, and actors bow after a performance. *Heterophones* have the same spelling but different meanings and different pronunciations, like *moped* (as in sulked) and *moped* (as in scooter).

- Words that are spelled the same but take on different meanings when capitalized are *capitonyms*, like *polish* and *Polish* or *nice* and *Nice*.

- *Hypernyms/hyponyms* indicate a more specific or more general relationship between words. For example, *duck* is a hypernym of *bird*, and *vehicle* is a hyponym of *car*.

- *Meronyms* describe a part of a whole indicated by another word. *Beak* is a meronym of *bird*.

- *Polysemes* are words with more than one similar meaning, like chair (something you sit on) and chair (person who leads a meeting).

If you want to dig more deeply into word meanings, have a look at WordNet, a lexical database maintained by Princeton University (http://wordnet.princeton.edu/).

USER-GENERATED CONTROLLED VOCABULARIES

Once again we'll look to LibraryThing, the innovative social cataloging Web site, for an example that mixes tagging with controlled vocabularies.

LibraryThing's "combine tags" feature lets users create an authority file for the site's tags. Any paying user can combine or separate two tags. For example, "science fiction" and "scifi" both refer to the same genre of futuristic literature; combining these tags makes them equivalent (see **Figure 4.3**).

Figure 4.3 Combined tags for "science fiction" on LibraryThing.

LibraryThing also uses popularity to confer authority. When tags are combined, the most popular tag becomes the preferred term.

Combining tags is guided by a simple rule—combining should be used only to eliminate meaningless differences between two tags. This leads to situations where some tags that seem identical—"humor" and "humour"—are not combined because they are seen to hold important differences. And, indeed, the list of books tagged with "humor" includes more American authors such as David Sedaris, Scott "Dilbert" Adams, and Jon Stewart, although "humour" leans heavily toward Douglas Adams and Terry Pratchett.

In other cases, the subtle cultural differences between two seemingly synonymous tags have been ignored. For example, the tag "science fiction" and its Spanish equivalent "ciencia ficcion" have been combined.

The validity of these distinctions is left up to the LibraryThing community. By giving its users control over combining and separating tags, LibraryThing enables an ongoing conversation about differences between tags. If LibraryThing's users agree that "humor" and "humour" are essentially the same, they can be combined, and the system reflects the decision immediately.

Taxonomies

A *taxonomy* is a controlled vocabulary that establishes parent-child, or broader and narrow, relationships between terms. Taxonomies are typically hierarchical (see **Figure 4.4**). They can define the hypernym-hyponym and meronym-holonym relationships between words (discussed in the sidebar "What's in a Word?"). They can also be used to define broader and narrower concepts, such as philosophy and epistemology.

The most famous taxonomy is probably the Dewey Decimal Classification system. Dewey designed a system with 10 top-level categories, followed by 10 subcategories, followed by another 10 subcategories.

In Dewey's classification system, each book is assigned to a single category. In most libraries you'll find Stephen Hawking's *A Brief History of Time* at 523.1 in the Astronomy and Space Sciences category.

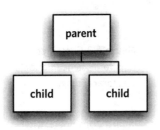

Figure 4.4 In a simple taxonomy each node has only one parent node but can have zero, one, or more child nodes.

Dewey set out to organize all human knowledge into his taxonomy, but most taxonomy efforts have more modest goals. Many Web sites use a taxonomic structure for their content. Companies, especially large ones, often maintain a corporate taxonomy for their records.

Most taxonomies provide a hierarchical, one-thing-in-one-place model that mirrors the real world. Amazon.com's product taxonomy give us an example of *polyhierarchy*—where an object can be placed on multiple branches of the taxonomic tree (see **Figure 4.5**).

Finally, the thesaurus is like a taxonomy on steroids. It combines broader, narrower and equivalence relationships along with associative ones, allowing you to traverse a hierarchy by jumping between related concepts as well as browsing up and down. Associative relationships can capture more subtle connections between words and concepts, like actions and their outcomes ("writing" and "book") or subjects and objects ("epistemology" and "knowledge").

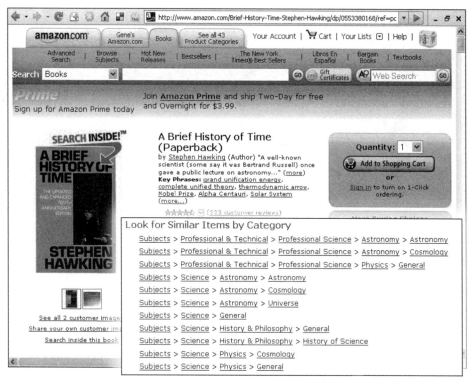

Figure 4.5 Amazon.com's polyhierarchical product taxonomy places *A Brief History of Time* in 11 categories.

Let's turn to some examples of tags and taxonomies working together.

ETSY: NAVIGATING WITH TAGS AND CATEGORIES

Etsy is an e-commerce site for people to buy and sell handmade goods (discussed briefly in Chapter 1). Because most of the items sold on Etsy are unique, it would be difficult to develop a complete set of product categories for the site.

However, buyers and sellers both benefit when products are easy to find. And browsing through categories is a useful—some would say an essential—way to discover products in an online store.

To resolve this tension, Etsy (see **Figure 4.6**) defines a set of top-level categories for its site such as "art," "children," "clothing," and "geekery." The subcategories are not predefined; they are based on tags added by users when they list a product.

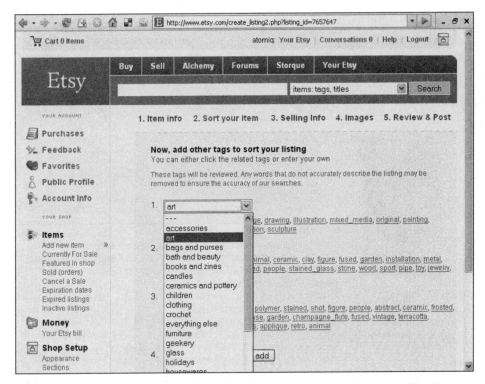

Figure 4.6 When listing a product on Etsy, users first choose a top-level category, then they add tags to describe the product.

The Etsy team moderates the tags—that is, they review them manually—before turning them into subcategories.

This hybrid approach ensures that Etsy's navigation system is stable and consistent at the top levels, while allowing subcategories that adjust to the contributions of Etsy's users.

THE BUBBLE-UP APPROACH: ENRICHING TAXONOMIES WITH TAGS

You don't have to create a taxonomy from tags to get value from mixing these metadata methods. Yahoo researcher Tom Coates has suggested a technique called *bubble-up folksonomies* that uses tagging to enrich an existing taxonomy, rather than trying to derive a taxonomy from tags themselves.

Here's how the bubble-up approach works: tags are attached to a resource, such as a song. Those tags are then "bubbled up" from several songs to describe their parent item, such as an album. Album tags are then bubbled up again to describe the artist. This retains the semantic relationship between resources while capturing the descriptive terms of users (see **Figure 4.7**).

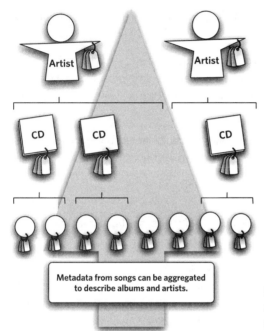

Figure 4.7 Tags attached to a song can be bubbled up to describe albums and artists.

The bubble-up approach is surprisingly common. Technorati, the blog search engine, bubbles up tags from individual blog posts to describe blogs. LibraryThing also employs a bubble-up approach when it comes to tagging its books. Each book in your LibraryThing collection is individually tagged. LibraryThing maintains a database of works, which are collections of individual editions of books. The tags you apply to your specific edition of a book are bubbled up to the work level.

Facets

Faceted classification is a way of organizing things by their relevant properties. Indian librarian S. R. Ranganathan invented faceted classification in the 1930s. Ranganathan understood that purely hierarchical classification systems were limited. His faceted classification allows objects to be classified along multiple dimensions and found via multiple paths.

But faceted classification didn't flourish until the Web. Web sites such as Wine.com and Epicurious.com introduced the first widely available examples of faceted classification. Since then, companies such as Siderean and Endeca have developed sophisticated faceted classification and browsing tools.

Some tagging systems—such as product reviews site Buzzillions.com—are leveraging faceted classification to boost the semantic value of their tags.

Understanding Facets

Imagine you run a clothing store. You have dozens of pants, shirts, and jackets on your racks. Every one of them comes in multiple colors and sizes.

You could organize your store in several ways. You could group your clothes by size, so people who wear a small could shop in one part of the store without being bothered by irrelevant sizes. You could organize your clothes by color, putting the black pants by the black shirts. Or you could organize by garment type, keeping all the pants together and separate from the shirts.

(Most clothing stores aren't designed to optimize the findability of a particular garment. They're designed to maximize the chance you'll buy something, which sometimes means keeping you in the store longer by making things harder to find.)

If you think of all the clothes in your store, you can see that they share a number of properties—such as size, material, garment type, and color. For each of those properties, we could come up with a number of values, like so:

- Garment type: blouse, skirt, jacket, pants, shirt
- Color: heliotrope, azure, honeydew, sunflower, glacier
- Size: S, M, L, XL
- Material: cotton, wool, rayon, silk

In a faceted classification system we would classify each garment based on these four properties and their values. You could also create an online store that allowed your customers to find a garment by exploring any of these properties. The result would look something like **Figure 4.8**.

Facets provide your users with many ways of finding any item.

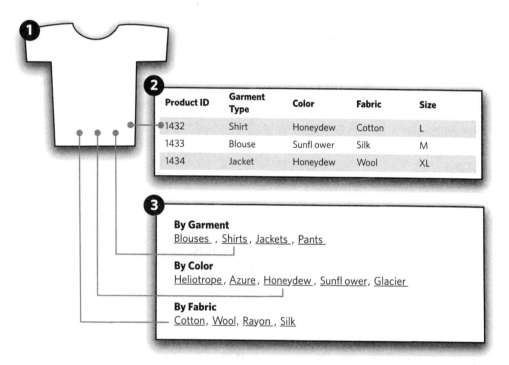

Figure 4.8 In our sample faceted classification scheme, a T-shirt (1) is classified by its properties (2). People can then browse our online store (3) by any of those properties to find the shirt.

Two Approaches to Faceted Tagging: Buzzillions.com and Mefeedia

Many people have observed that the same basic kinds of tags—such as people, resource types, places, and events—appear in most tagging systems. Once you've noticed these patterns, it seems like a natural step to separate tags by type. In other words, to separate them into facets.

Creating facets for tags has several potential benefits:

- Facets help make tags more precise. If you have a facet for people, you can be confident that the tag "Helena" in that facet isn't a reference to Helena, Montana.

- Facets can improve findability and make browsing easier by grouping tags into clearly delineated concepts.

- Facets let you make connections between kinds of tags—such as people, places, and events—that might not be visible otherwise.

Faceted tagging typically differs from regular faceted classification in that facets are predefined, but the facet terms are not. Because the facet terms are tags, the number of terms will grow as long as people continue to add tags.

Buzzillions.com and Mefeedia take the idea of faceted tagging in two slightly different directions.

BUZZILLIONS.COM

Buzzillions.com mixes tagging, facets, and taxonomies to create a product reviews site that uses reviews to make it easier for people to find products.

Reviews are great for evaluating a product you already know about, but they're not great for discovering something new. (Adding ratings can help you learn about new products—such as the most highly rated products in a category.)

Buzzillions.com is interesting for two reasons:

- It uses structured reviews, so instead of writing a few paragraphs about a product, you use tags. These tags then become part of navigation on Buzzillions.com and help other users find the products in which they're interested.

- Buzzillions.com integrates several different approaches to classification. Taxonomies, tags, and facets all play a role in its product reviews.

Let's look more closely at how Buzzillions.com uses tags.

There are four facets for each product review: Pros, Cons, Best Uses, and Describe Yourself. You can enter any number of tags for each facet, but Buzzillions.com suggests some common tags depending on the kind of product you're reviewing. For hiking boots, for example (see **Figure 4.9**), the suggested tags are "comfortable," "durable," "great traction," "non-slip sole," "stable," and "water-resistant." These tags are presented with check boxes, making it easy for you to select them.

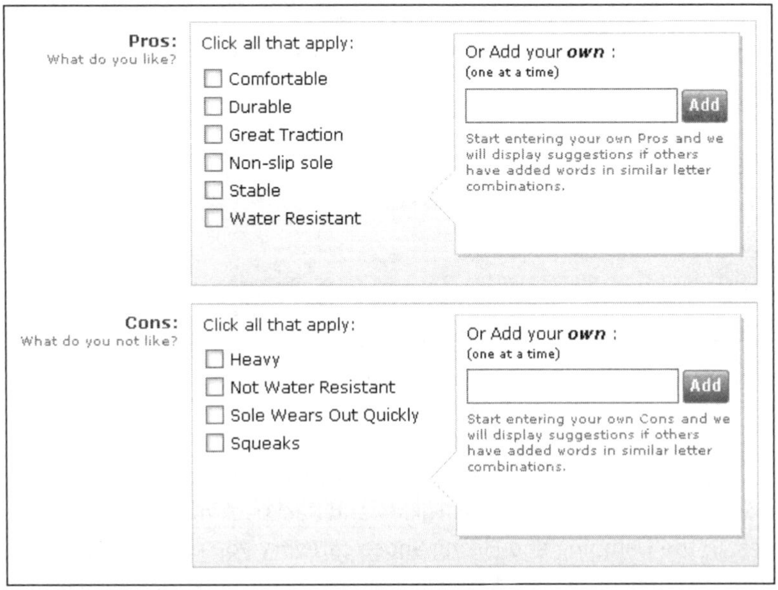

Pros:
What do you like?

Click all that apply:
- [ ] Comfortable
- [ ] Durable
- [ ] Great Traction
- [ ] Non-slip sole
- [ ] Stable
- [ ] Water Resistant

Or Add your *own* :
(one at a time)

[   ] [Add]

Start entering your own Pros and we will display suggestions if others have added words in similar letter combinations.

Cons:
What do you not like?

Click all that apply:
- [ ] Heavy
- [ ] Not Water Resistant
- [ ] Sole Wears Out Quickly
- [ ] Squeaks

Or Add your *own* :
(one at a time)

[   ] [Add]

Start entering your own Cons and we will display suggestions if others have added words in similar letter combinations.

Figure 4.9 The tagging interface at Buzzillions.com gives users suggestions based on the product being reviewed, as well as the opportunity to add their own.

Buzzillions.com also displays mini tag clouds for different products to help you select a product. Selecting a tag (see **Figure 4.10**)—in this example, "avid adventurer"—will filter the results to just those that have the selected tag. If you choose a Con, Buzzillions.com will filter out all the products that have received that tag.

Figure 4.10 Choosing (1) "avid adventurer" and (2) "great traction" filters the list of results (3) to just the boots that have those two tags.

Buzzillions.com's product catalog also uses a taxonomy. You'll find hiking boots in the category Sporting Goods > Camping, Hiking and Backpacking > Camping and Hiking Shoes. In the Camping and Hiking Shoes category you can also narrow the product choices by gender or brand, or you can select subcategories such as Crampons and Mountaineering and Ice Climbing.

What makes Buzzillions.com impressive is how seamlessly it's integrated these three distinct kinds of classification. The taxonomy helps you get to the right product category. The tags and facets help you narrow your choices in that category based on criteria that are meaningful to you. It's a slick system that accelerates your transition from browser to buyer.

MEFEEDIA

Mefeedia (http://www.mefeedia.com) is another Web site that uses faceted tags. Mefeedia aggregates *vlogs*, or video blogs, from around the Web. Video blogs are short digital videos created by bloggers and shared using blogging technology.

Mefeedia's faceted tagging is much simpler than Buzzillions.com's tagging system. Each tag on Mefeedia can be assigned to one of five facets: events, language, people, places, and topics. Tags can also be left unassigned.

A human approach was used to assign tags to facets. Mefeedia founder and information architect Peter Van Dijck went through the most popular tags and chose a facet for each of them. "It was quite easy to do the top 1,000 tags, actually," he says, "it only took a few days."

Users can browse Mefeedia by facets and tags (see **Figure 4.11**). Each facet is given its own tag cloud. Each tag also has its own wiki page where users can, if they choose, discuss how it's used.

Figure 4.11 A sample of Mefeedia's faceted browsing interface.

THREE PRINCIPLES FOR MIXING TAGS AND FACETS

Van Dijck has three principles for marrying tags and facets:

- **Always be easy**. Tagging should remain as easy as possible.

- **Baby steps**. A little semantics can give you a lot of leverage when it comes to creating useful structure from tags.

- **The work of the few impacts many**. Just like Wikipedia is edited by a few users, a few users assigning tags to facets can create a valuable structure for other users.

"I notice a hesitance toward hard-coded semantics and manual work—people think these things won't scale," says Van Dijck. "I learned to mix it up...a small amount of semantics on top of minimal structure with a little manual work can work wonders."

Folksonomies

Folksonomy has become a popular term to describe the bottom-up classification systems that emerge from social tagging.

But what kind of classification structure is a folksonomy?

Other classification systems define relationships—broader, narrow, equivalent, related—between terms or between concepts referred to by terms. In a folksonomy, the relationships between tags are inferred based on their usage patterns. There are no formal relationships in a folksonomy, other than perhaps "degree of relatedness."

Because a folksonomy uses algorithms to look at tagging patterns, two tags that have no known semantic relationship (like "blowfish" and "sql") may have a statistical relationship.

Let's look at a couple of examples. Assume we have a collection of bookmarks in Del.icio.us. Two hundred of those are tagged with "webdesign," 200 are tagged with "css," and 200 are tagged with "ajax." Some of the "css" bookmarks are tagged with "webdesign" and "ajax," some of the "ajax" bookmarks tagged with "webdesign," and "css," and so forth (see **Figure 4.12**).

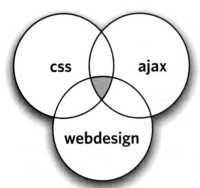

Figure 4.12 Bookmarks tagged with "css," "webdesign," and "ajax."

What can we say about the semantic relationship between these three tags? We can guess, based on how much they overlap, that they are related in some way. If you were familiar with "webdesign" and you'd never heard of "ajax," you might guess correctly that "ajax" is a new technology or tool related to "webdesign."

If you work on the Web, you already have an intuitive sense of how these three terms are related. But consider a slightly different example, taken from the social bookmarking site Connotea. **Figure 4.13** shows how three different tags—"ccr5," "hiv," and "cxcr4"—overlap for a collection of bookmarks.

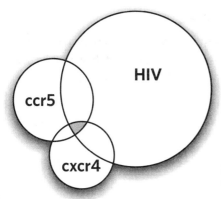

Figure 4.13 Resources tagged with "ccr5," "hiv," and "crcx4."

How would you describe the relationship of these tags? You might know that CCR5 and CRCX4 are coreceptors for the HIV virus. You might guess that because they appear together frequently (but not always) that they're related. But without a prior knowledge of the domain, it would be difficult to understand the semantic or conceptual relationship between these terms based just on their use.

Even if two tags were used in concert all the time by a wide variety of users across multiple resources, we couldn't make any claims about them other than that they are highly related (see **Figure 4.14**).

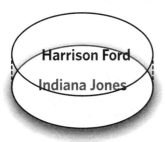

Figure 4.14 In a hypothetical tagging system the two tags "Indiana Jones" and "Harrison Ford" co-occur 100 percent of the time. Can we say they're equivalent?

In reality, semantics are much more nuanced than statistics. But don't let that diminish your interest in folksonomies. The malleability of words—their ambiguities, connotations, implications, and double entendres—is what makes language fun. And it's also part of what attracts people to tagging.

Four Characteristics of Folksonomies

So folksonomies are not like other classification systems. A folksonomy doesn't involve the broader-narrower relationships that characterize taxonomies. And they can't be said to establish equivalence between terms the way a controlled vocabulary does.

In a folksonomy, the relationship between tags is inferred based on how the tags are used. This is one of four key characteristics of folksonomy:

- Tagging is done independently.

- Tags are aggregated.

- Relationships are inferred.

- Any inference method is valid (though some are better than others).

INDEPENDENCE

To create a folksonomy, users must be free to choose their own tags. They should not be forced to choose from a limited list of preselected categories.

Some tagging systems offer suggestions—a tool aimed to help users add tags more easily and efficiently. Earlier in the chapter we saw that Buzzillions.com, for example, provides users with a list of suitable tags they can choose for each product.

These systems still meet the criteria for independence as long as users can still add their own tags.

AGGREGATION

Aggregating the tags of many users creates a folksonomy. *Aggregation* means pulling all the tags together in an automated way. Sampling tags to manually create a taxonomy, for example, is different from a folksonomy. (Etsy's approach to building categories from tags might fall outside this definition of folksonomy.)

How many users do you need to create a folksonomy? It depends on the size of your tagging system, but if you have an active community of participants, then you'll probably see interesting folksonomic patterns. On the other hand, aggregating the tags of a few users, or inactive users, may not produce patterns that are useful to you.

INFERENCE

Unlike other classification systems, a folksonomy doesn't establish a particular kind of semantic relationship between tags. The relationships between tags are inferred from their use.

The value of these derived relationships is that they're based on the language and usage patterns of real users. They might lack the nuances of the semantic structures described earlier, but they're grounded in real user behavior.

MANY METHODS OF INFERENCE

There are many ways to analyze tags to infer semantic relationships.

- Counting tags to see which is most popular is the simplest way of examining tagging patterns.

- Co-occurrence counts which tags are used together. For any given tag, you count the frequency that other tags have been used with it, which gives you a list of statistically related tags. Co-occurrence loosely approximates the associative relationship in a thesaurus.

- Clustering is an algorithm that looks at the co-occurrence of two tags and calculates the probability that they will appear together. Clusters of tags are then calculated by grouping the tags that have a high probability of co-occurrence (see the sidebar "Clustery Goodness" for more details).

All of these techniques have been used in other fields, and there is nothing distinctly folksonomic about any of them. For example, they could be used to analyze keywords from a controlled vocabulary. What makes a folksonomy is applying them to tags added by users on their own for their purposes.

WHEN TO USE FOLKSONOMIES

So far in this chapter we've looked at examples where tagging is merged with other kinds of classification. But folksonomies can be valuable on their own.

Here are five situations where folksonomies work well:

- **Nomenclature is uncertain or evolving**. When the language that defines a domain is changing (as Timo Hannay discusses in Chapter 2), regular classification schemes aren't possible. Folksonomies can provide some structure in their place.

- **Dynamic information space**. When the information space you're trying to organize is highly dynamic—growing or changing rapidly—folksonomies can help you keep pace with those changes.

- **Semantic relationships aren't critical**. When the semantic relationships built into other kinds of classification aren't necessary, the user-generated structure in a folksonomy may be good enough.

- **Multiple viewpoints are desirable**. While other classification systems reflect a single point of view, folksonomies can capture the perspective of the multitudes.

- **You can tap into an active base of users**. Folksonomies depend on an engaged community of users who continually add tags. Without these users, you can't have a folksonomy.

So, is that all there is to folksonomies? Not quite.

I chose to define folksonomy narrowly for this book so I could compare it to other ways of organizing things. But for some people the term *folksonomy* encompasses a lot more—maybe everything to do with tagging. If you prefer the broad definition of folksonomy, you'll find more information on tag clouds, popularity-driven navigation, and other topics in Chapter 5.

Tags in the Metadata Ecosystem

Classification systems are not without their problems. They can be slow to change. They reflect, and reinforce, a particular worldview. They are rooted in the culture and era that created them.

They can also be absurd. In the ICD a runner that's hit by a car falls into the same category as a swimmer hit by a car. You'd think there are some pretty important differences between those two events.

The people who create classification systems have not been ignorant of these issues. *Sorting Things Out*, by Susan Leigh Star and Geoffrey Bowker, discusses the cultural biases behind many popular classification systems (including the ICD). David Weinberger's book *Everything Is Miscellaneous* has an excellent discussion of some of the arbitrary and silly categories made in the Dewey Decimal Classification system.

Sandy Berman, a cataloger at the Hennepin County Library in Minnesota, spent more than 30 years trying to make the Library of Congress subject headings more usable and less biased. Just one example of Berman's contributions is the subject heading "apartheid," which he added to the Hennepin County Library in 1973. The Library of Congress added it in 1986, well after the worldwide movement to end apartheid had begun.

Note

Find out more about Sandy Berman at http://www.sanfordberman.org/.

The Metacrap Problem

For some people, the problem is not just classification systems but metadata itself. In "Metacrap: Putting the torch to seven straw-men of the meta-utopia," author and activist Cory Doctorow tells us why metadata is often, well, crap.

Part of Doctorow's critique is leveled at the people who create metadata (and these days that's all of us): we are lazy, stupid, dishonest, and self-ignorant. And if you think about it, that's largely true. We don't follow instructions; sometimes we can't spell and punctuate properly; and we often aren't the best judges of our own information. These facts make all metadata somewhat suspect (tags, too).

But Doctorow also makes a persuasive case that classification systems aren't all they're cracked up to be. Doctorow says, "requiring everyone to use the same vocabulary to describe their material denudes the cognitive landscape, enforces homogeneity in ideas. And that's just not right."

Note

You'll find "Metacrap: Putting the torch to seven straw-men of the meta-utopia"
at http://www.well.com/~doctorow/metacrap.htm.

Clustery Goodness

Clusters are an algorithmic approach to grouping tags. Clustering analyzes how frequently tags appear together, to infer their relationships.

Clustering is one of the best ways to glean tag relationships. When tags are frequently used together, there's a high likelihood they're related. The relationships created by clustering algorithms are most like the semantic relationships—broader, narrower, and equivalence—we've discussed so far in this chapter.

Flickr offers the best-known example of what it calls *clustery goodness* (see **Figure 4.15**), but others have implemented clustering as well.

Figure 4.15 Flickr's clusters separate photos tagged with "turkey" into distinct groups: photos of the country Turkey, photos about Thanksgiving, and photos about birds.

Clustering involves several steps:

1. Counting the number of times tags co-occur for a particular set of resources

2. Calculating the probability of two tags occurring together

3. Grouping the high-probability terms together into clusters

Though it's more complicated than other approaches, clustering produces patterns that approximate our semantic relationships. In their paper "Automated Tag Clustering: Improving Search and Exploration in the Tag Space," Grigory Begelman, Philipp Keller, and Frank Smadja outline some of the challenges with clustering:

- **Ambiguity**. Sometimes words have distinct senses that can't be teased out through a clustering analysis. For example, "library" might mean a collection of programming functions or a place where books are stored.

- **Community**. Different communities can have different tagging patterns, so a tag might cluster differently depending on the community of taggers.

- **Longevity**. People's tags change over time, so today's clusters may not be relevant tomorrow.

Despite those challenges, clustering remains one of best ways of extracting meaning out of tagging patterns. A word of caution, though: clustering is not simple to implement. You will need someone comfortable with statistics and computer programming to use this method.

Clay Shirky picked up on this idea and suggested that even simple synonym rings unfairly homogenize the world. His widely cited example is the difference between "movies" and "cinema." To a cataloger these appear to be similar concepts, but the people who use these terms have entirely different perspectives on film. It's the same for "queer politics" and "homosexual agenda."

Here is where tags can help. They don't force existing categories onto users, and they encourage use of a natural vocabulary. But they're also messy and can miss even the most common-sense semantic relationships between terms.

The Middle Problems

Shirky levels another criticism at classification systems: they don't scale, and they can't keep up with the world. They may work well for smaller, stable collections of documents. But they can't operate at the scale of the whole Web.

The most insightful comment I've read on this topic comes from Karl Fast, a professor of information architecture at Kent State University. On an information architecture mailing list, Fast compared the kind of structure created by librarians to the Web-scale structures created by search engines such as Google:

> Classic LIS (library and information science) believes that to achieve order and facilitate retrieval a minimum amount of structure must be *imposed* on the document space. The Web falls well below the necessary baseline that classic LIS would say is necessary.
>
> What Google does is *derive* higher orders of structure from a document space that is a chaotic mess when viewed from the perspective of classic LIS principles. So when librarians attempted to catalog the Web based on AACR2, it was a massive failure. It was too big, too chaotic, and too dynamic. Your only option is to derive structure.
>
> And that is what Google did. Their insight was to embrace the structure of the Web and figure out how it could be exploited to facilitate retrieval. Where LIS said, "How can we make the Web like our classic systems?" Google said, "We can't change the Web, but maybe we can find some useful properties and exploit them to build a better retrieval system."
>
> I'm not arguing against structure. I'm simply pointing out that the question of structure is actually several questions: What form of structure? How much structure? How does it get created? And, how can we use this structure to facilitate retrieval?
>
> We tend to think that the hard problems are the big ones. So we believe that searching the Web is hard because it's so huge. But I've been thinking lately that the really hard problems are actually the ones in the middle. In the middle, many algorithms don't work that well with moderate document sets, context becomes much more important, interaction is critical, and you can't get the user "in the ballpark" anymore—you have to get them to right to the thing they're looking for.
>
> *—Karl Fast*

Both Fast and Shirky agree that when it comes to organizing information, scale matters. Interestingly, most of the examples in this chapter are of small-scale tagging systems. It remains to be seen whether tagging will work as a way of organizing the whole Web.

The Pace-Layering Problem

Another perspective on this topic is that tags, taxonomies, and facets represent different speeds of classification.

Pace layering is the theory that aspects of society change at different rates. Pace layering was first promoted by Stewart Brand, author of *How Buildings Learn*, who conceived of fast-moving layers such as fashion and commerce revolving around slow-moving layers such as culture and nature.

Thanks to Peter Morville, pace layering has found its way into the world of metadata (see **Figure 4.16**). In his book *Ambient Findability* Morville suggests that metadata structures such as taxonomies are stable and long-lasting, while tags are more fast-moving and volatile.

> For quite some time, I have believed this concept of pace layering holds great promise within the narrower domain of Web design. In this discussion of metadata, the potential for a unifying architecture is self-evident. Semantic Web tools and standards create a powerful and enduring foundation. Taxonomies and ontologies provide a solid semantic network that connects interface to infrastructure. And the fast-moving, fashionable folksonomies sit on top: flexible, adaptable, and responsive to user feedback.
>
> —*Peter Morville*

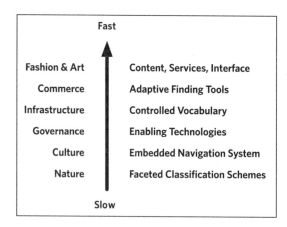

Figure 4.16 On the left, Stewart Brand's concept of pace layers in society. On the right, Peter Morville's pace layers of information architecture.

Although it's true that tagging works well in our fast-moving stream of information, tags can also work on the slower and more stable layers.

We don't have to look further than the Buzzillions.com example earlier in the chapter to see that tags can be a first-class form of metadata. In the Buzzillions.com system, tags are performing a unique and meaningful role that complements their product taxonomy. In this case tags are not, as Morville suggests, simply feedstock for more enduring classification systems.

Studies of Del.icio.us have also shown that tagging patterns are more stable than they might first seem. Tagging patterns for individual resources achieve equilibrium in a relatively short period of time. This suggests that tagging systems can offer some of the consistency offered by Morville's slower layers (without the same kind of semantic relationships).

An Ecological Solution

Information scientists Grant Campbell and Karl Fast examined pace-layering theories of metadata from an ecological perspective in their paper "From Pace Layering to Resilience Theory: The Complex Implications of Tagging for Information Architecture." They say, "Seeing systems as ecologies emphasizes the interaction of players over the stratification of layers."

Their analysis yields some interesting conclusions about the impact that tagging might have on more traditional information structures. They note, for example, that a destabilizing force—such as tagging—can promote the long-term survival of the ecosystem by maintaining diversity. They also observe, reflecting Clay Shirky's criticisms of taxonomies, that some ecosystems achieve a false stability that reduces their ability to adapt to changes.

One intriguing proposition is that the librarians, information architects, database designers, and other professionals who create taxonomies and controlled vocabularies could "reposition themselves as guardians, not of a system's architectural stability, but of its ecological resilience... Such a role relies less on the metaphor of architecture and more on the metaphor of urban planning."

We can imagine the information architects of the future spending more time at the edges, managing the emergent properties of folksonomies alongside the semantic relationships of taxonomies. We can hope that the polarizing debates over folksonomies versus taxonomies and imposed structure versus derived structure are over. The examples in this chapter point to a future where tags, taxonomies, and facets interact to create new and valuable information structures.

Summary

- Tagging is an approach to collecting metadata. Metadata is "documentation for your data."

- Tags can be grouped into seven tag types: descriptive, resource, ownership/source, refinement, opinion, self-reference, task organizing, and play and performance.

- Controlled vocabularies include synonym rings and authority files. A "combine tags" feature can allow users to create an authority file for tags.

- Taxonomies have parent-child relationships between nodes. Tags can enrich taxonomies by being "bubbled-up" from lower levels to higher ones.

- Folksonomies have four features: users can add any tags they choose; all tags are aggregated; relationships between tags are inferred; and there are many possible methods of inference.

- Folksonomies work best when language is uncertain or evolving, when the resource collection is changing quickly, when semantic relationships aren't critical to users, when multiple points of view are desirable, and when you have an active base of contributors.

5 Navigation and Visualization

WHAT YOU'LL LEARN IN THIS CHAPTER:

- Everything you ever wanted to know about tag clouds
- Navigating tag space through pivot browsing, popularity, and filtering
- Geotagging—combining tags with geographic data

Once your tagging system is set up, you have to think about how your users will find information within it. What tools will you give them for navigating their tags or the tags of others?

Tags are unlike other kinds of navigation. There's no up or down, no top or bottom, and in many cases no categories or facets to anchor the information. Navigating through tags is often a process of sifting rather than moving deliberately to a specific destination.

In this chapter, we'll look at how you design navigation for the tag space. We'll also examine ways of visualizing tags—in particular, the tag cloud—to help people make sense of tag data.

Tag Clouds

By now you're familiar with tag clouds. You've already seen a dozen or more of them in this book.

With the growing popularity of tagging, tag clouds have become a fashionable way of displaying tags. But like any fashion, what's hot today can look like an embarrassing fad tomorrow. In a popular and oft-quoted blog post last year, Web designer Jeffrey Zeldman referred to them as the mullet of Web design.

Still, their chicness aside, tag clouds can be valuable:

- They're an easy-to-create visualization.

- They show the zeitgeist of your tagging system.

- They can act as navigation, creating an interesting entry point for browsing the resources and users in the system.

In the following sections, we'll focus on how tag clouds work and how they can be used. You can decide whether they're appropriate for your project.

Tag Clouds: The Basics

Let's look at a simple tag cloud: Flickr's all-time most popular tags (see **Figure 5.1**). The cloud consists of approximately 150 tags listed in alphabetical order. The size of each tag varies according to how popular it is.

Figure 5.1 Flickr's most popular tags—one of the first (if not *the* first) tag clouds.

If we dig under the hood a little, we'll find some interesting properties of tag clouds. The first thing to notice is that the size of the tag is not directly proportional to the popularity of the tag.

Figure 5.2 shows the size of three popular tags from Flickr—"wedding," "architecture," and "rome"—along with the approximate number of photos for each tag. The row labeled "To-Scale Size" shows you the approximate size of the tags relative to the actual number of photos (using "rome" as the base size).

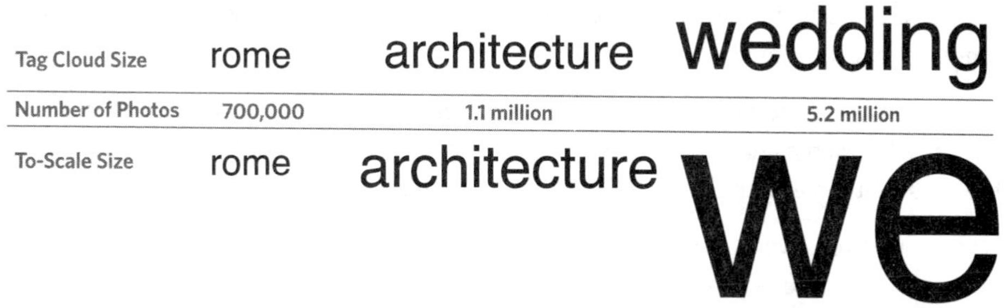

Tag Cloud Size	rome	architecture	wedding
Number of Photos	700,000	1.1 million	5.2 million
To-Scale Size	rome	architecture	we

Figure 5.2 The popular tags from Flickr. Tags are scaled down so they're readable in the tag cloud.

Keep in mind that the tags in Figure 5.2 are three of the most popular tags on Flickr. There are millions of other tags that have been used less frequently. Remember the "squaredcircle" example we looked at in Chapter 2? That tag has been used some 60,000 times—but that's not frequent enough to appear in Flickr's most popular tag cloud. If it did appear, its to-scale size would be roughly 1/10th of the tag "rome."

If tag sizes were scaled based strictly on their frequency, some tags would be huge, while others would be tiny. And you know from Chapter 3 that tag frequencies often follow a power-law distribution—a few tags are used with great frequency, while most tags are used infrequently.

Let's talk about how you make a tag cloud that doesn't have dozens of inscrutably small tags and a few gigantic ones.

Making a Tag Cloud

Creating a tag cloud requires two things at a minimum:

- A list of tags
- A count of how frequently each tag appears

In most cases you'll query a database to come up with a list of tags. The first decision you'll face is how many tags to include in your cloud. Flickr, Del.icio.us, and Yahoo's MyWeb 2.0 show about 150 tags.

But the right number for you will depend on how much space you have to display your tag cloud. If you plan on filling up a whole Web page, a large number may be appropriate. If you're placing tags in a sidebar, then a smaller number such as 30 to 50 may be better.

The tagging patterns in your system will also be a factor. If there are a few very popular tags and many infrequently used tags, you may end up with tags used just a few times in your tag cloud.

One easy way to drop those occasional tags from your tag cloud is to require that each tag be used a certain number of times. You might tell the database to return only the tags that have been used, say, five or more times.

Once you've retrieved your list of tags, it should look something like what's shown in Table 5.1. (These tags are a sample of my Del.icio.us tags; the count numbers are taken from Del.icio.us too.)

Table 5.1 Sample Tags and Frequency Counts

Tag	Count	Tag	Count	Tag	Count
design	120	gaming	23	science	5
ux	68	google	14	lists	4
ia	65	tv	14	innovation	3
socialsoftware	54	culture	12	miscellaneous	3
tags	46	comix	7	complexity	3
web2.0	43	statistics	6	facets	3
business	34	art	5	networks	3

The next step is to decide on the scale of your tag cloud. It's a choice that lies at the intersection of aesthetics and mathematics—you have to design a formula that creates the tag cloud you want.

If your tag patterns are typical—if they follow that power-law curve—you will face a trade-off between *legibility* (can people read the smallest tags?) and *accuracy* (does the size of the type reflect its frequency?). In most cases, the right decision will be to choose legibility; you'll want your users to be able to read the tags.

So, how do you avoid the problem illustrated in Figure 5.2? It's all about scaling—you use a scaling formula that sizes your tags between a minimum and maximum font size. You might decide that your least popular tags are displayed at a minimum font size—say 12 pixels tall—and your most popular tags are no larger than a maximum font size. In this case we'll pick a maximum font size of 48 pixels so the largest tags don't overwhelm the smallest ones.

Note

The type sizes you actually choose may depend on the design of your interface.

Now you need to consider how you'll scale the tags between those sizes. There are many ways to do this, but we'll focus on two methods: proportional scaling and linear scaling.

PROPORTIONAL SCALING

The easiest way to scale your tag cloud is to use some simple algebra to convert your tag counts to percentage or pixel values. We'll call this *proportional scaling,* since the size of the tag is directly proportional to its count—within the upper and lower pixel bounds we set.

The basic idea behind proportional scaling is to measure the distance between our least popular and most popular tags and then compress it so it fits between the pixel boundaries we set. The formula that does this scaling is simple, and it's covered in detail in Chapter 7.

This leads to a tag cloud that has features similar to the power-law curve mentioned earlier—a few large tags and many small ones. Using proportional scaling, the tags from Table 5.1 would turn into a tag cloud like the one shown in **Figure 5.3**.

Figure 5.3 A tag cloud created using proportional scaling.

LINEAR SCALING

Another method is to flatten out the power-law curve using a mathematical function called a *logarithm.* We'll call this approach *linear scaling,* meaning that the differences between the smallest and largest will be linear rather than exponential.

The math involved in linear scaling is slightly more complicated—but not much. Because virtually every programming language has a logarithm function, the extra programming effort is just a few keystrokes.

Figure 5.4 shows the tag cloud generated with linear scaling.

art **business** comix complexity culture **design** facets **gaming** google **ia** innovation lists miscellaneous networks science **socialsoftware** statistics **tags** travel tv **ux** web2.0

Figure 5.4 A tag cloud created using linear scaling.

So, which method should you use? Aesthetics are always subjective, but linear scaling seems to produce a more attractive tag cloud that's easier to read. Another benefit, if your tag cloud doubles as navigation, is that your tags will be generally larger and thus easier to click. For example, you can see that tags such as "business" and "comix" are much larger in Figure 5.4. (This is because linear scaling makes tags in the middle of that distribution larger than proportional scaling.)

However, if accuracy is important to you or your users, you might consider a proportional scaling approach.

These choices assume that your tags follow a power-law distribution. If they don't, you should try both methods and see which produces better results based on your own data (see **Figure 5.5**).

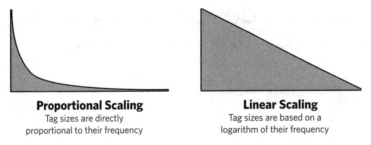

Proportional Scaling
Tag sizes are directly proportional to their frequency

Linear Scaling
Tag sizes are based on a logarithm of their frequency

Figure 5.5 Proportional scaling can result in a few large tags and many small ones. Linear scaling lifts the middle of the distribution to even out the differences.

Expanding Tag Clouds

Information architect Joe Lamantia calls tag clouds "the camera obscura of the semantic landscape." In other words, each tag, resource, or user is a small porthole into the whole information space.

We've just covered the simplest tag clouds, but there are a variety of other ways to widen that porthole and make tag clouds more interesting and potentially more useful.

ADD BASIC CONTROLS

You might consider adding controls so users can sort the tag cloud, such as an option to view the tags alphabetically or by frequency. You might also add controls, such as a slider so users can adjust the number of tags shown in the interface.

DISPLAY MORE DATA

You can also add more data into the cloud. For example, you might show the number of times a tag has been used. Some tag clouds use variations in color along with size to indicate how frequently a tag has been used.

In its popular tag cloud, Del.icio.us shows you which tags you've used out of the most popular tags (see **Figure 5.6**).

school **science** **search** security seo sga shopping slash social software teaching tech **technology** **tips** tools **toread** travel tutorial tutorials tv **ubuntu** video videos web web2.0 webdesign webdev wiki **windows** wishlist wordpress writing youtube

(red tags are tags you share with everyone else)

Figure 5.6 Del.icio.us colors the tags you've used red, while the other tags are blue.

ADJUST THE TIME SCALE

When something is tagged is almost as important as *how* it is tagged.

We can't say for sure whether tags become less accurate, or meaningful, as they age. But when we look at tag data from different time spans, we can see interesting differences in the tags.

Varying the time span of a tag cloud can reveal important nuances about people's tagging behavior (and help users discover interesting resources that they might not otherwise find).

Take Flickr's popular tags as an example. Flickr offers two time-limited tag clouds on this page: popular (hot) tags in the past 24 hours and over the past week (see **Figure 5.7**).

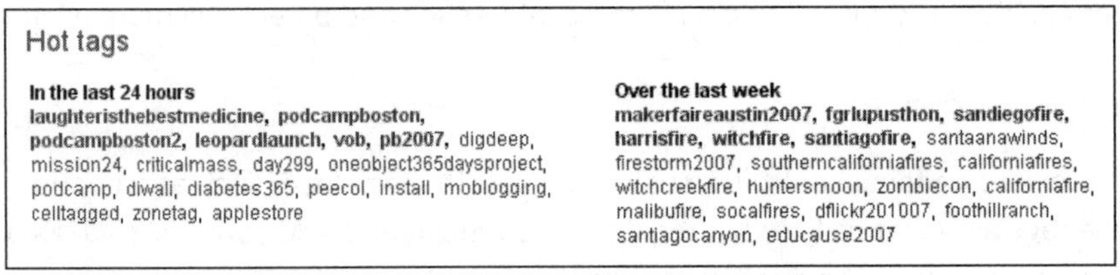

Hot tags

In the last 24 hours
laughteristhebestmedicine, podcampboston, podcampboston2, leopardlaunch, vob, pb2007, digdeep, mission24, criticalmass, day299, oneobject365daysproject, podcamp, diwali, diabetes365, peecol, install, moblogging, celltagged, zonetag, applestore

Over the last week
makerfaireaustin2007, fgrlupusthon, sandiegofire, harrisfire, witchfire, santiagofire, santaanawinds, firestorm2007, southerncaliforniafires, californiafires, witchcreekfire, huntersmoon, zombiecon, californiafire, malibufire, socalfires, dflickr201007, foothillranch, santiagocanyon, educause2007

Figure 5.7 The one-day and one-week mini tag clouds on Flickr's popular tags page.

Notice how the tags change as the time frame shortens. Many of the most popular recent tags are for events—conferences, workshops, and festivals. These aren't popular enough to appear in the most popular tag cloud, which is dominated by general tags like "weddings" and "sunset."

But they're the most common tags for a short period of time. Tags with a short burst of popularity may be more relevant for some users than the all-time most popular tags.

ADD MORE INTERACTION

Most tag clouds are simply a thin layer of navigation on top of other content. Once you click a tag, you're taken to a list of resources with that tag. One way to make a tag cloud more interesting is to let people explore tag space within the cloud itself.

Phillipp Lenssen created a drill-down tag cloud using the tags from Andy Baio's popular blog. Clicking a tag loads a list of posts tagged with that term. The list appears in-line, becoming part of the tag cloud itself. (You can view the drill-down tag cloud at http://blogoscoped.com/waxy/.)

Another interesting interactive tag cloud is Moritz Stefaner's elastic tag map (see **Figure 5.8**). This Flash-based visualization shows relationships between tags, as well their frequency of occurrence. The elastic part comes when you click a tag and the cloud pulls together related tags and connects them with arcing lines.

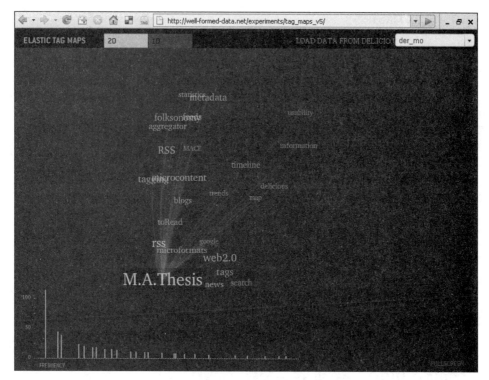

Figure 5.8 Moritz Stefaner's elastic tag maps visualize the relationships between tags. Note the frequency graph at the bottom left, which approximates the power-law curve.

Elastic tag maps are just one of several visualizations Moritz created to address some of the challenges faced by simple tag clouds:

- Tag clouds emphasize the popular tags at the expense of interesting but more infrequent tags.

- They sum up tagging activity over time without addressing the dynamics of activity.

- They don't show the relationships between tags.

To address these issues, you need more sophisticated techniques for tag analysis as well as better visualization tools (elastic tag maps were built in Flash). You can see more of Moritz's visualizations at http://well-formed-data.net/thesis.

BUT THINK FIRST

Before adopting these solutions, you have to answer a larger question about the purpose of your tag cloud. Is it merely a gateway to other content? It is a summary of tagging trends? Or is it the backbone of your navigation system?

Most tag clouds are part visualization and part navigation, a veneer on top of other navigation systems. In these cases, simple tag clouds, plus a control or two, are fine. If you have greater ambitions for your tag clouds, then investing in advanced features will be worthwhile.

You could also consider alternative methods of presenting tags, for example, as a list or as an alphabetical index (see **Figure 5.9**). The tag cloud is a popular solution, but it's not the only one.

The other kinds of navigation you use should also influence your choices for tag clouds. We'll look at tag navigation in the next section.

Figure 5.9 Yahoo's MyWeb2.0 offers multiple views of its tags: as a cloud, an alphabetical index, and more.

Navigating Tags

Navigating—clicking links to explore an information space—is probably the most common activity on the Web. And designing navigation is certainly one of the most common aspects of Web design.

But navigating through a tagging system is a different experience than navigating the information structures we discussed in Chapter 4. Browsing a hierarchy, for example, often means moving through more general to more specific categories (or vice versa). Browsing a faceted system involves combining facets to constrain the number of items from which we have to choose.

Tagging systems aren't designed from the top down; they're built from the bottom up through the collective efforts of their users. As a user, if you're looking for an answer to a particular question, you might find dozens of resources that meet your needs (and each of them might be tagged differently). As a designer, you're challenged by not knowing exactly what resources people will add or what tags they'll use.

Your job, then, is to create a framework for navigation that supports these differences. That's why navigation in tagging systems tends to take three forms: pivot browsing for exploring the system, popularity-based navigation for understanding the dynamics of the system, and filtering for drilling into the data efficiently.

Pivot Browsing

Pivot browsing means moving through an information space by choosing a new reference point—a *pivot*—for exploring the system.

The power of pivot browsing lies in how it allows you to explore information along multiple dimensions—how it's categorized, who is using it, and how it relates to other information. At any time during that exploration you can switch, or pivot, to look at a different dimension.

PIVOT POINTS

A collaborative tagging system has three potential pivot points: the user, the tag, and the resource. Every time a link is saved in Del.icio.us, for example, metadata about the user, the resource, and its tags are stored. This metadata can be connected to other metadata—saved by you or by other users—to let you explore for related information.

You can pivot on the user who posted it to view their tags and resources. You can pivot on any one of the tags to find other bookmarks with the same tags. Or you can pivot on the bookmark to see who has saved it and what tags they've used (see **Figure 5.10**).

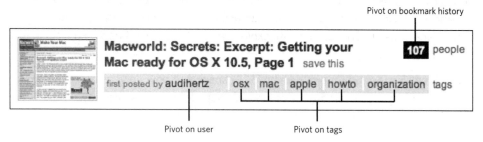

Figure 5.10 Pivot points for one resource in the Del.icio.us interface.

DESIGNING FOR THE PIVOT

In Figure 5.10 you can explore all three dimensions of the system, but there's a slight emphasis given to tags. There are five tag links compared to just one each for users and resources.

The goal of the pivot is not to guide people to specific content but merely to give them many paths to discover information. But it will be important for you to consider which dimension will give your users the most value.

For example, you could re-imagine Figure 5.10 in a way that brings more focus to users or resources. **Figure 5.11** is one way to emphasize users instead of tags.

Macworld: Secrets: Excerpt: Getting your Mac ready for OSX 10.5
posted by gsmith, atomiq, huckabees , jernigan , mrdarcy and 102 others
tags: osx, mac, apple, howto, organization

Figure 5.11 Changing the pivots for a bookmark to emphasize users. The important question to ask is, "What will people get the most value from exploring?"

Note

If you have other metadata that intersects with your users, resources, or tags—such as ratings or groups—you could also include that as a pivot point. Amazon.com's tag pages allow you to pivot to lists and discussions as well as products.

One factor that's consistent among all our examples is that every interface is link-rich. This is generally a good thing—each link acts as another porthole on the entire information space and gives people a new pivot point to consider.

Like any other design project, you should still consider your users' needs, follow good interface principles, and evaluate the interface with real users before you launch. These link-dense interfaces facilitate exploring, but if they're not designed well, they can be overwhelming.

Pivot browsing is good for prospecting in tag space, but how do you know what to look for while you're exploring? This is where popularity comes into play.

Popularity

In your day-to-day life you probably use popularity as one way to judge the quality, value, or importance of the information you encounter. You might look at the best-seller lists to find a book, or you might check out the opening weekend box office numbers to help you pick a movie. In some cases you'll use popularity along with other information—such as the opinions of friends and experts—to help you figure out what's interesting.

The same idea applies in a tagging system: popularity can be a valuable metric for judging the quality or importance of resources in a tagging system.

We've already looked at tag clouds, which show us the most popular tags in the tagging system. We can also use popularity measures to reveal other interesting information in our system—such as resources that have received the most tags or users who have added the most resources.

TIME AND POPULARITY

When you look at popularity, however, you quickly run into a problem with *all-time* popularity: it doesn't change much. Just like there's a good chance you've seen many of the all-time most popular movies, you've probably also seen the all-time most popular resources in your tagging system.

Once again, the power-law curve we discussed in Chapter 3 comes into play. The most popular item will be many times more popular than an item of average popularity. And that means it will take a long time for any average item to unseat the most popular items—if it ever does.

When you design popularity-driven navigation, it's important to consider time as a significant component of the design. Using a short slice of time will reveal popularity patterns that aren't apparent from the all-time perspective (as you saw in Figure 5.7). If your users are particularly active, you might look at time slices as small as an hour. If not, a day or week might be a sufficient time span to show current tagging activity.

TRENDS

Changes in popularity are sometimes just as interesting as popularity itself. Part of the appeal of Billboard's Hot 100 popular music chart is that it tracks gainers and losers as well as the current chart position for any given song. It lets you know what's becoming popular, which is arguably as important as knowing what's popular now. After all, everyone wants to be ahead of the popularity curve.

In a tagging system you might track the popularity trends of resources (which ones have been added) or tags (which are gaining and losing).

Both of these approaches can help users discover resources that are new and interesting. It can also help people connect activity in the tagging system to other events in the real world.

PERSPECTIVES ON POPULARITY

In addition to time and trends, we often want to know what's popular among different groups of people. These different perspectives on popularity can help us identify the things we're interested in—or at least help us narrow down that stream.

Consider these four ways of looking at what's popular in a tagging system:

- **You**. Understanding your own popularity trends can help you identify changes in your interests and your information-seeking patterns.

- **Friends or contacts**. These are the people who share your interests. Knowing what's popular with them is, in a way, like reading your own mind. Del.icio.us's network feature (covered in the social bookmarking case study) is an example of tracking your friends.

- **Team or workgroup**. For an internal tagging system—on an intranet or extranet—your teammates' popular tags and resources can help you stay on top of your business.

- **Everyone**. The most popular items overall are always interesting. Global popularity provides a good reference point for your own tastes even if the most popular items don't appeal to you. (Most tagging systems include just a small subset of everyone, so we're talking about everyone *in the system*.)

Popularity-driven navigation is better when it allows contrasts between these perspectives. Like trends and time, the differences in these perspectives are as valuable as they are individually.

DEALING WITH THE VOCAL MINORITY

In Chapter 3 we talked about the vocal minority problem: when a small number of active taggers seem to take over your system. The problem is not that there are active taggers; it's that the actions of a few people are seen to represent the whole community.

The vocal minority problem is endemic to systems with popularity-driven navigation because most popularity algorithms don't adjust for a user's activity.

You can combat this problem in a few ways:

- If you have just a few highly active taggers whose tags are not typical, you could manually exclude them from your popularity algorithms.

- Take the figure-skating approach. Just like the highest and lowest scores are dropped when calculating a skater's final score, you could exclude the tags of the most frequent taggers in your popularity count. Your system would then reflect the behavior of people in the middle, not the outliers.

- When you're calculating tag popularity, reduce the weight of tags that have been added many times by the same user. In essence, you're saying that a tag entered 10 times by one user is worth less than a tag entered 10 times by ten users.

All of these approaches come with a downside. Most popularity algorithms are quite simple to implement. Each of these suggestions will be harder to put into place. Nonetheless, if the vocal minority is a problem in your tagging system, one of these solutions might help balance your popularity-driven navigation.

Filtering

Generally speaking, filtering is the process of separating the stuff you don't want from the stuff you do want. In a tagging system, filtering is a way of separating the users, resources, and tags that interest you from everything else.

Pivot browsing is a way of filtering—navigating through a system by isolating one element at a time. But more sophisticated filtering systems can combine two, three, or more pieces of metadata to narrow the number of choices you see.

TAG COMBINATIONS

The most common approach to filtering involves letting users combine multiple tags to locate resources with just that set of tags. In fact, tag combinations are one of the best ways to reduce a stream of information to a trickle that can be easily consumed.

In some ways, tag combinations are like search. People have to identify the tags they're interested in—the ones they think will produce the results they want—and then enter them. Unlike typical Web searches, most tag combinations will look for only the tags entered. They won't expand the tags to include plurals or other commonly used forms.

Still, tag combinations are a good way of letting people drill down into your system using just tags. In the social bookmarking case study, we'll look at how Del.icio.us lets you combine tags to filter out unwanted bookmarks.

LIBRARYTHING'S TAGMASH

LibraryThing provides a clever way to combine tags called TagMash. TagMash lets you look for books with a particular combination of tags, but its filtering algorithm also lets you de-emphasize or negate tags by using the minus sign. A single minus sign, such as in "-fiction," will simply de-emphasize the tag "fiction." A double minus sign, such as in "--fiction," will exclude books tagged with "fiction" from the results (see **Figure 5.12**).

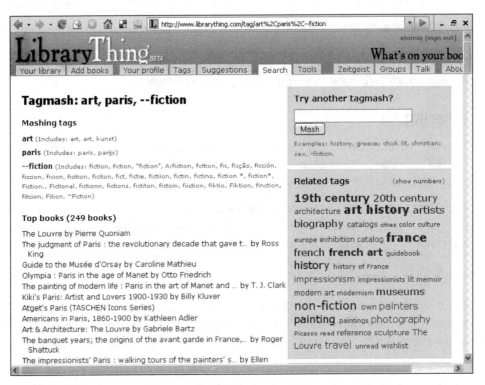

Figure 5.12 A TagMash of "art," "paris," and "--fiction."

A TagMash page for "19th century," "romance," and "--fiction" will find every book tagged with "19th century" and "romance" except those that are also tagged with "fiction."

TagMash is a semiautomated system—users define the interesting groups of tags, while TagMash mashes them together and comes up with a list of titles.

One benefit of TagMash is that ambiguous tags can be clarified by combining them with other tags. The tag "leather," for example, is applied to leather-bound books, to books about leather crafts, and to a subgenre of erotica. Users interested in just leather-bound books can subtract or negate tags such as "crafts" and "erotica" in their TagMashes.

Unlike some of the approaches we discussed in Chapter 4 that sought to understand semantic relationships between tags through statistics, TagMash relies on users to come up with combinations that fit their interests. If the TagMash doesn't work—if it includes books they don't want or excludes books they do—they can just create a new TagMash.

Geotagging

Geotagging means adding geographic tags, such as latitude and longitude or place names, to resources. Geotagging can be applied to all kinds of resources, but the example we'll focus on in this section is Flickr.

Unlike other tags, geotags require a particular kind of structured metadata—geographic coordinates—to place resources on a map. Those coordinates can be derived from existing tags such as place names, or they can be entered directly by users.

Both approaches have been used with Flickr photos, and that's part of what makes the geotagging story interesting. The early attempts at geotagging came from outside Flickr. Developers began playing with Flickr's tags and feeds—as well as emerging tools such as Google Maps—to see how they could use maps to navigate photos.

Mappr was an early attempt to geolocate photos based on their tags (see **Figure 5.13**). After Mappr came other Flickr/maps mashups, including a site called Geobloggers (see the interview with Mike Migurski for more of that story).

Geobloggers introduced a tagging convention that would eventually be adopted by Flickr for placing photos on a map. Geotagging involves adding three special tags to a photo:

- A marker tag, "geotagged," that identifies photos with location tags

- A latitude tag in the format "geo:lat= 53.54109"

- A longitude tag in the format "geo:lon=-113.49761"

These last two tags are called *triple tags*, or *machine tags*, and they're a way to provide machine-readable data inside a tag (see the "Machine Tags" sidebar for more information).

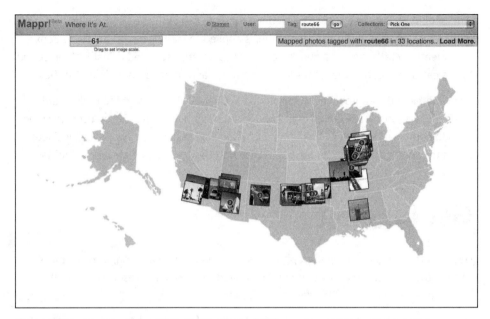

Figure 5.13 In Mappr, photos tagged with "Route 66" formed a path from Chicago to Los Angeles, just like the real Route 66.

Geobloggers scanned the RSS feed for the tag "geotagged" and extracted photos with machine tags for latitude and longitude coordinates. It then placed those photos on Google Maps.

THE VIRTUOUS CYCLE OF TAGS AND FEEDS

In Chapter 2 we talked about how tags and feeds—acting as a simple read-write system for Web applications—could drive innovation. Geotagging is one of the best examples of this phenomenon.

Tags give people a way to add longitude and latitude data to the system. Feeds give people a way to extract that data. In this case, just the photos that are marked with the tag "geotagged."

Some of the services built out of this fairly simple system were eventually incorporated into Flickr itself. And in addition, the machine tag convention was generalized to work in a number of applications. For example, you can find many photos with machine tags from Yahoo's event-tracking Web site Upcoming. Upcoming (http://upcoming.yahoo.com) uses these tags to pull photos from events into its pages.

Mike Migurski: Mappr, a Flickr/Maps Mashup

This is an interview with Mike Migurski, the director of technology at Stamen Design.

How did Mappr work?

Mappr examined the tags that people use on their Flickr photos and made educated guesses about where in the world those photos may have been taken. We did our best to process the fire hose of Flickr photographs as they were posted, without requiring that photographers specifically ask to have their photos geotagged. The project was designed as a thought experiment. We did the tag-matching to illustrate a possible future where digital cameras with built-in GPS were commonplace.

Was Mappr the first Flickr/maps mashup? If not, what inspired you?

To my knowledge, it was. We were inspired by other non-map Flickr mashups, though, and guided by our earlier map work for clients such as MoveOn.org. Flickr's API had been released in autumn '04 and spawned a flurry of experimentation. We released Mappr a short time later, in December '04.

How did you match tags to latitude and longitude coordinates?

Mappr's guesses were made by comparing the complete tag set for a given photo to a database of U.S. place names (states, counties, cities, and ZIP codes) and applied a heuristic confidence rating to its guesses—a photo tagged "SF" and "California" was considered very likely to have been taken in San Francisco, while a photo tagged "Concrete" might well have been taken in Concrete, Washington, but we didn't put much faith in that guess. The more specific a user's tags were, the better we did at figuring out where the photo was taken.

A while after Mappr launched, Dan Katt released his Geobloggers site, which allowed users to tag their photos with specific geographic tags by pointing out their precise location on a Google map. The photo would get a tag like "geo:lat=37.00," which eventually became a natively supported feature of Flickr after Dan was hired into the company. Aaron Cope and Dan generalized this feature into the machine tags "context:key=value" Flickr sports today.

Three years ago, the difference between the two approaches was huge: Mappr was a passive experience for users, while Geobloggers was an active one. Now, with GPS units in cell phone cameras becoming commonplace and Flickr supporting geographic features directly, we think that explicit geocoding might just "fall out" of taking photographs with the right kind of camera. This is a more Mappr-like experience, where the management application you use figures out where you took the photograph automatically, instead of you having to point at a map.

None of this could have happened without an open tagging system and feeds for each tag. What's most interesting about this story is that tags and feeds together created a virtuous cycle. Ideas and infrastructure for geotagging were built using these simple tools, and then more sophisticated implementations were created once the ideas were proven.

Flickr has moved to more polished techniques for adding geographic data to photos. Users can now drag and drop their photos on maps and have the place coordinates added automatically—without having to wrestle with machine tags.

Machine Tags

Machine tags are a convention for creating tags that can be processed and understood—and even created—by computers. Machine tags are also interesting because they can be very precise, and they can be used by other applications or Web sites. And like regular tags, they don't need to be predefined (although there are standards emerging).

Figure 5.14 shows the three parts of a machine tag—the namespace, key, and value—along with some sample tags. Machine tags are similar to the faceted classification systems we discussed in Chapter 4. If you recall the online clothing store example from that chapter, we could apply a machine tag—such as clothing:size="large"—to a garment to approximate faceted classification. In this case, the namespace is equivalent to the domain ("clothing"), the key to a facet ("size"), and the value to a facet property ("large").

Machine tags gained traction at Flickr, where you can even search for machine-tagged photos through its API. For more about machine tags, visit http://machinetags.org.

Figure 5.14 Machine tags follow a common "namespace: predicate=value" format, but they don't have to be predefined.

TAGS, MAPS, AND METADATA

Other services continue to bring together tags and maps in interesting ways. TagMaps, for example, combines tags, maps, photos, and tag clouds in one interface. You can explore photos of a place such as San Francisco (see **Figure 5.15**) by clicking a tag cloud overlaid on a map. At a high level, the tags are a surprisingly good overview of the city and its notable features.

Selecting a tag such as "Alcatraz" will display a handful of photos of the famous prison, all taken by Flickr users. Through clever use of metadata, TagMaps can even let you view photos taken at night.

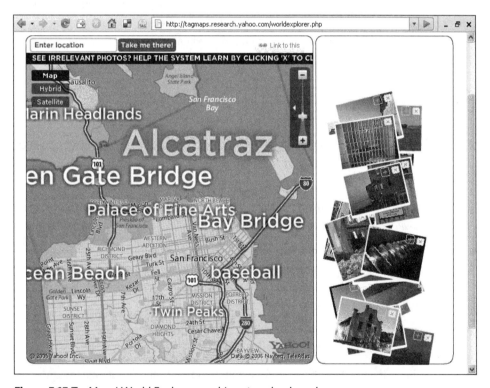

Figure 5.15 TagMaps' World Explorer combines tag clouds and maps.

TagMaps was created by Yahoo Research Berkeley. So far this book has focused on tagging digital and Internet-based resources. With geotags we're branching out into annotating physical space, and that forces us to ask some interesting questions about data and metadata. Are geotags metadata about the photo? Or is the photo metadata about the place represented by the tags?

You've probably heard the expression "The map is not the territory." But what happens when the map—metadata about the territory—and the territory bleed together? Some start-ups have experimented with tagging locations from mobile phones. At Foundcity (http://foundcity.net), for example, you tag places by sending an address and tags from your mobile phone.

As GPS devices become embedded in mobile phones, it will only get easier to tag and add digital metadata to physical locations. You'll be able to query that data too, combining tags to locate the best Italian restaurant or the nearest dry cleaners, or by zooming backward in time to view the history of a place in tags.

Whether these systems support the particular kind of tagging we've discussed in this book remains to be seen. But it seems likely that they'll offer collaborative metadata of some kind—and many of the lessons from tagging will apply.

Summary

- Tag clouds are a popular and simple way to visualize tag data. Creating a tag cloud is easy—you need only a list of tags and how frequently they appear in your tagging system.

- Pivot browsing lets you explore the tag space by pivoting—using a tag, resource, or user as a vantage point for viewing a particular slice of data in the tagging system.

- Popularity is a valuable metric for assessing the value of information. In a tagging system, popularity-driven navigation can help users identify the resources that are most interesting to others. Popularity trends are often more important than all-time popularity.

- Filtering resources based on multiple tag combinations can be a highly effective way of zooming in on a small set of resources.

- Geotagging is the practice of adding geographic data to resources through tags. Map-based browsing can be a great way to find resources. More important, geotagging is a concrete example of how tags and feeds can launch a virtuous cycle of innovation.

6 Interfaces

WHAT YOU'LL LEARN IN THIS CHAPTER:

- Patterns for tagging interfaces

- Character- and action-delimited tagging interfaces

- Three kinds of tag suggestions and how they influence tagging activity

- Approaches to editing, deleting, and moderating tags

Given that most tagging interfaces are a single text input box (see **Figure 6.1**), you might wonder why we're spending a whole chapter talking about them. Are they really that important?

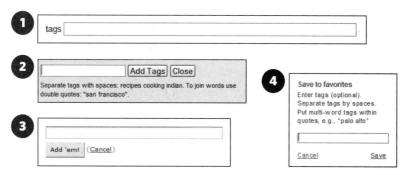

Figure 6.1 Four tagging interfaces: (1) Del.icio.us, (2) 43 Places, (3) Technorati, and (4) SlideShare.

The simplicity of that one box belies its importance. The choices you make around it—such as size, delimiters, and suggestions—will impact all of the tagging that happens in your system.

In this chapter, we'll look at how to design tagging interfaces, and we'll discuss how those design choices affect the tagging system overall.

Tag entry and management—how the tags get into the system and how we change them once they're in there—are two key parts of tagging interfaces. We'll also consider suggestions and discuss the pros and cons of influencing people's tags.

Patterns in Tagging Interfaces

As you learned in Chapter 2, there are many reasons people might tag, including future retrieval and contribution, and sharing with a community of interest. You will probably have your own goals for your tagging system, such as creating community or helping people find the resources they need. These different—and sometimes competing—needs must be balanced by the tagging interface.

You can look at tagging interfaces as a mix of two patterns: one based on the action the user is performing and one based on the number of resources the user is performing the action on.

- **Action**. Users can add a resource to the system and provide tags for it at the same time (which we call *adding and tagging*), or they can tag resources that already exist (*just tagging*).

- **Resources**. They can perform these actions on just one resource (*individual tagging*) or on many resources at once (*bulk tagging*).

Figure 6.2 shows how these patterns complement each other. And as you'll see, many systems offer more than one pattern (and some offer all four).

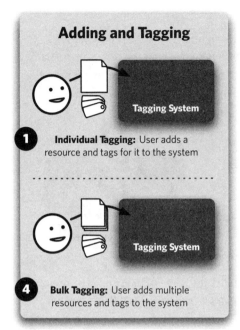
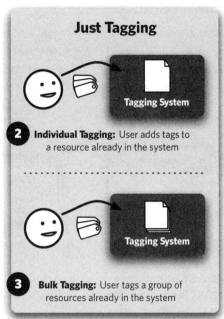

Figure 6.2 Four modes of adding tags, clockwise from top left: (1) Adding and tagging one resource, (2) just tagging one existing resource, (3) just tagging multiple existing resources, and (4) adding and tagging multiple resources.

Adding and Tagging Resources

Add-and-tag interfaces serve a dual purpose. Their primary function is to add a resource—such as a photo or a bookmark—to a system. The secondary purpose is to save some descriptive information about that resource, such as a title, description, and tags.

Tags are just one possible (and often optional) element of add-and-tag interfaces. Users can also add a title, a text description, and other metadata that helps them identify the resource. Connotea, a social bookmarking application for scientists, lets users store complete citation data when they add a paper to the system (see the social bookmarking case study in Appendix A for more on this).

Add-and-tag interfaces allow users to contribute both resources and tags simultaneously. Not only is this easy for users, but it's also good for the system overall—more resources and more tags make the system more valuable to other users. (Sometimes tagging is optional; users can add tags and resources at the same time, or they can add tags later.)

BOOKMARKLETS

One convenient way of accessing an add-and-tag interface is via a *bookmarklet*. Bookmarklets are small applications built into a bookmark on the browser toolbar. Clicking the bookmarklet launches the application that, for example, might save the current Web page to your favorite social bookmarking tool (see **Figure 6.3**).

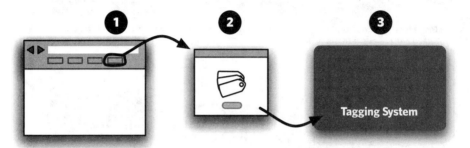

Figure 6.3 Anatomy of a typical bookmarklet: (1) click the bookmarklet to open a pop-up window, (2) add tags and other metadata in the pop-up window, (3) and then save that data to the tagging system.

Bookmarklets come in different flavors. Social bookmarking site Ma.gnolia offers four versions of its bookmarklets: one that opens in the same page, one that opens in a pop-up window, a mini version, and a simple mark-it-for-tagging-later version.

Having more than one option is probably good considering that users have different reasons for tagging. You should recognize, though, that a simple save-it-and-forget-it interface will probably generate fewer tags (as well as titles and descriptions) overall. Tagging seems to work best when people can do it right when they're saving the resource.

Bulk Tagging

While add-and-tag interfaces such as bookmarklets operate on one resource at a time, bulk tagging involves assigning tags to two or more resources at once. Bulk tagging most often appears when users are adding a group of resources as a batch—such as importing bookmarks from a browser into a social bookmarking tool or using a desktop application to upload a group of photos at once.

Bulk tagging accelerates the tagging process by letting users efficiently tag many resources at the same time. But its convenience may come with a cost. Bulk tagging might encourage people to use generic tags that apply to the whole batch, rather than specific tags that identify each individual resource.

Ideally you hope that people will use a two-step process: use bulk tagging to apply common tags to all resources in the batch and then add specific tags for each individual resource (or the important ones anyway). But that may not be possible, or even realistic.

Nonetheless, bulk tagging is an important feature, especially when your users need to add many resources at once. Some tags are better than none.

Just Tagging (Existing Resources)

Tagging will often involve resources that already exist in your tagging system. This might be because users have already added them, or it might be because the resources come from somewhere else entirely.

Amazon.com is a good example of "just tagging" resources that are already part of a system—in this case the system is Amazon.com's product catalog.

Amazon.com has a long history of using social features to help sell products. It was one of the first online stores to use suggestions based on customer purchasing patterns. It was also an early pioneer of user-generated content with its Listmania feature.

In late 2005 Amazon.com introduced a tagging module to its product pages. Amazon.com customers can add tags to any product—even if they don't own it. But more important, at least for this discussion, is that the users can't add resources to the system. Amazon.com's catalog is essentially closed.

Despite this, tagging serves a valuable function at Amazon.com: connecting you to products and helping you organize the products that interest you within Amazon.com's vast catalog.

PUTTING ALL FOUR PATTERNS TO WORK

Earlier we mentioned that these patterns aren't mutually exclusive. At least one site, Flickr, has used all four (by now that shouldn't be a surprise):

- Flickr offers a Web interface for uploading and tagging photos one by one.

- Flickr's Uploadr utility can save multiple photos to Flickr, and you can tag them as a batch from your desktop (see **Figure 6.4**). Tens or even hundreds of photos can be added to the system and tagged at the same time.

- Flickr has an organizer interface that lets you tag batches of photos you've already added.

- And you can always tag existing photos, right from the photo page.

Why are there so many ways to tag photos? People take hundreds of photos at a time now, so bulk uploading and tagging is practically a necessity. Tagging in Flickr is equal parts participation and organization, so it only makes sense that Flickr would embed tagging throughout the application.

Note

Read the media sharing case study in Appendix B for more information about tagging photos, videos, and other rich media.

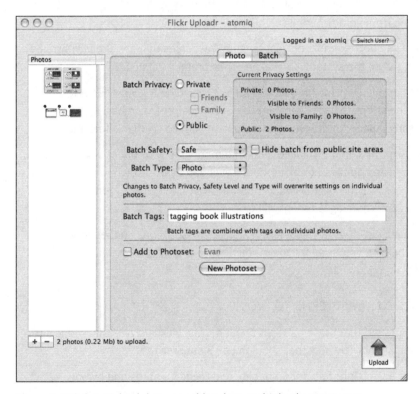

Figure 6.4 Flickr's Uploadr lets you add and tag multiple photos at once.

Tag Entry

We've looked at a number of tagging interface patterns that share common features. Let's focus now on the particulars of how tags get into the system.

You're already familiar with the single text input box, but that's not the only way users can enter tags. There are other interfaces for entering free-form categories, and they provide a good foil for our study of tagging interfaces.

Speed and Simplicity

Categories in Microsoft Outlook bear more than a passing resemblance to tags (see **Figure 6.5**). You add categories to the master list and then assign multiple categories to each e-mail. There are no restrictions on the categories you can enter; what's good is what works for you.

Blogging software Movable Type also has categories that are functionally similar to tags. You can create new categories right from your blog post, and you then assign a post to as many categories as you want.

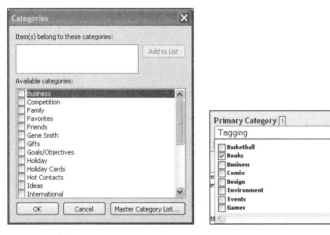

Figure 6.5 On the left, categories in Microsoft Outlook; on the right, categories in Movable Type (recent versions of Movable Type have included tags as well as categories).

Although these interfaces offer functionality similar to tagging systems, they don't *feel* like tagging. There's too much friction—too many clicks, too much interaction—and that tells us something important about tagging.

Tagging interfaces are characterized by *speed* and *simplicity*. They encourage users to quickly list relevant keywords—underscoring the point that tagging is not meant to be time-consuming—with a bare minimum of interaction.

Tags also have an appealing ad hoc quality. You can use a tag just once and not have to see it again in a list of categories every time you go to tag something. This encourages a kind of extemporaneous categorization that you don't see in typical category systems, even when they resemble tagging in a functional way.

The goal of most tagging systems is to make it easy for people to enter tags. So tag entry usually involves a text box, often just a single line, where users type their tags and submit them.

Many tag entry interfaces look the same, but there are some important differences. One fundamental difference is whether the interface is character-delimited (where tags are submitted in a group, like at Del.icio.us) or action-delimited (where tags are submitted individually, like at Amazon.com).

Character-Delimited Systems

In character-delimited systems, users type several tags into a text box—separated by a special character called a *delimiter*—and submit them all at once. Because these interfaces tend to be minimal, you have just a few design decisions to make. They boil down to the size of the text box, the delimiter, and how you handle features such as suggestions (if you offer them).

THE SIZE OF THE BOX

A text box is a text box, right? Not quite. The size of the text box is a way of telling users how many tags you expect they'll enter. One study of tagging patterns in Del. icio.us showed that tagging frequency dropped after people had entered seven tags. Researchers suggested that the size of the text box is a cue to people about the number of tags to enter.

One simple rule of thumb is that a larger box encourages a greater number of tags. A smaller form field, in contrast, appears to limit the number of tags a user can enter.

DELIMITER

The next thing to consider is the delimiter. In this case the delimiter will be a keyboard character—such as a space, semicolon, or comma—that the system will use to tell tags apart. It could be any character, and there's nothing particularly special about it on its own. In fact, you're probably already using delimiters when you send an e-mail to multiple people and you separate the e-mail addresses with a comma or semicolon.

Your tagging system, however, will use the delimiter to take a string of text like "johnnycash walktheline music movie" and turn it into a set of discrete tags like "johnnycash," "walktheline," "music," and "movie."

This work is done by a script that parses the text entered by the user and breaks it into individual text chunks whenever it finds the chosen delimiter.

Two common delimiters are spaces and commas:

- Del.icio.us uses spaces to separate tags. Spaces are fine delimiters until you want to tag something with multiple words or a phrase. For example, if you tagged a presidential speech on Del.icio.us with "George W. Bush," Del.icio.us would interpret this as three distinct tags: "george," "w.," and "bush." To create a single tag for "George W. Bush," you would have to use underscores, like "george_w_bush," or smash words together, like "georgewbush."

- Commas function just like spaces, but they allow people to enter multiword tags like "George W. Bush," "south america," or "ia summit" without extra effort. Other punctuation delimiters, such as semicolons, work in the same way as commas.

What kind of delimiter should you choose? Commas or spaces are probably fine, but you should make sure the delimiter is absolutely obvious to users. Commas have a slight advantage because they allow users to enter multiword tags naturally. But thousands of Del.icio.us users do fine with space-delimited tags.

Action-Delimited Systems

In an action-delimited system, tags are entered individually into the text field and submitted one by one. It's slightly more work for users, since they have to click each time they enter a tag. On the other hand, it's easier for users to understand how to separate tags.

An *action-delimited system* is one where a click, a key press, or any other user action determines the discreteness of a tag (see **Figure 6.6**). Action-delimited systems have the benefit of allowing a greater range of tags, including multiple words and phrases. And because the tags are separated by an action, users can include any character they want without worry.

Figure 6.6 Amazon.com uses action- and character-delimited tagging in its Tag this Product window.

However, because of the additional effort involved in tagging, these interfaces are most common in those "just tagging" situations where resources already exist.

TO CAPITALIZE OR NOT TO CAPITALIZE?

Regardless of which tag entry system you choose, give some thought to capitalization. It might seem trivial, but how you handle capitalization is important. Allowing capitals in tags means there can be multiple versions of a single tag term. The tag "technology," for example, could also be entered as "Technology," "TECHNOLOGY," or any other combination of uppercase and lowercase letters.

If your tagging system needs to handle capitals, consider keeping two versions of the tag: the original tag as it's entered and a standardized version that eliminates capitals as well as spaces, underscores, and other unnecessary characters. This helps keep your tag set tidy while allowing users to enter multiple versions of the same text string.

In Chapter 7 we'll look at FreeTag, a tagging plug-in that standardizes tag terms. Flickr does this as well, as you can see in **Figure 6.7**.

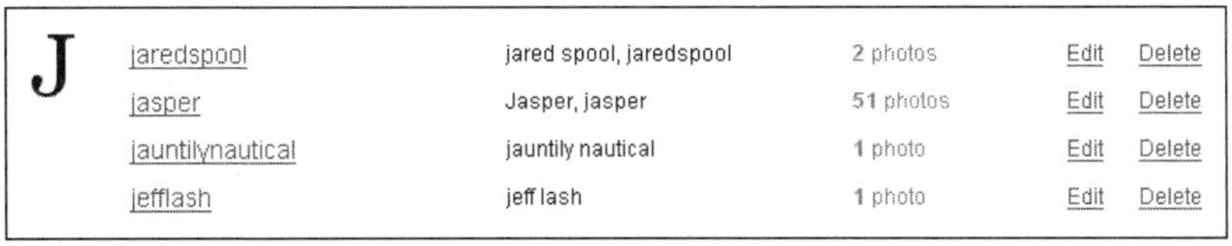

J	jaredspool	jared spool, jaredspool	2 photos	Edit	Delete
	jasper	Jasper, jasper	51 photos	Edit	Delete
	jauntilynautical	jauntily nautical	1 photo	Edit	Delete
	jefflash	jeff lash	1 photo	Edit	Delete

Figure 6.7 Flickr normalizes tags by eliminating spaces, capitals, and punctuation, but it keeps track of the original tag.

Suggestions

Many tagging systems make it easier for users by recommending tags. These tag suggestions have several benefits. For users, they can accelerate the tagging process by allowing them to pick from existing tags—either one of their own or one entered by another user.

Suggestions can also help reduce noise because of typographical errors, plurals, spelling variations, or acronyms. In several tagging systems, people actively use the tags "web 2.0," "web2," and "web-20"—all minor variations of the same concept. In most cases these kinds of distinctions are unnecessary, and suggestions can be a helpful way of reducing them.

Three Kinds of Suggestions

We can divide suggestion systems into three categories:

- **Previously used tags**. Tags that the user has entered already
- **Popular tags**. Tags that have been used frequently by others
- **Recommended tags**. Tags the user should consider based on popular tags, recently used tags, and other factors

PREVIOUSLY USED TAGS

Some suggestion systems are based strictly on tags a user has entered already. These systems can help users tag more accurately and efficiently—and keep them using a consistent set of tags.

Previously used tag suggestions are limited by the user's vocabulary, which means that they can never suggest new and potentially interesting tags. And it cannot help the user discover what other people are calling something.

POPULAR TAGS

Popular tags are chosen from the tags added by other users. When creating suggestions based on popular tags, you should consider the issues related to time and popularity discussed in Chapter 5. Here are three things to consider:

- **Source**. The source of the suggestions could be all the other users in the system, or it might be limited to just the users' contacts or groups. If your tagging system is quite tribal—where users form tightly knit and distinct communities—then popularity based on contacts or group membership could be valuable. The trade-off is that as you narrow the source of your suggestions, the number of suggested tags decreases as well, which can limit their value.

- **Scope**. Are you pulling tag suggestions based on the resource being tagged? This requires that at least one other person—and ideally several other people—have tagged that resource already. If that's not possible, you can broaden the scope and show popular tags for the whole system (or whatever subset of the system you've chosen as your source).

- **Horizon**. You could also attach time limits to suggestions so that only popular tags from the past day, week, or month appear. This kind of popularity horizon can be useful in situations where your resources change frequently or when people are tagging topical content (such as news stories).

In any case, popular tag suggestions bring a social element to the act of tagging. This can be incredibly helpful—we can learn new things about a resource by observing how others have tagged it. But it also brings social proof—discussed briefly in Chapter 2—into play.

RECOMMENDED TAGS

Recommended tags are a convenient but somewhat artificial bucket for other kinds of suggestions that mix popularity and previous use with other algorithms.

Why is the distinction between previously used, popular, and recommended tags significant? Well, you intuitively understand what *previously used* and *popular* mean. Recommendations are more opaque.

In some cases, like the Buzzillions.com example from Chapter 4, the recommended tags may be preselected. In other cases they may be determined by a formula—like the collaborative filtering algorithm Amazon.com uses for its "people who bought this also bought" feature.

Sticky Tags

One emerging approach to suggestions is *sticky tags*. Sticky tags stick to kinds of resources and appear automatically when a user tags that kind of resource in the future.

Wesabe, a personal finance Web site that tracks your spending to help you achieve your financial goals, pioneered sticky tags (see **Figure 6.8**). When you tag a bank account transaction or credit card purchase, you have the option to apply sticky tags or one-time tags. Sticky tags are automatically attached the next time you make a purchase from that merchant.

One potential benefit of this approach is that it can automatically handle obvious tags, letting you focus on more meaningful tags. Sticky tags are a way of anticipating your tagging patterns based on the kinds of things you tag—almost like letting you apply tags into the future.

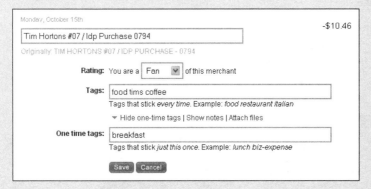

Figure 6.8 Wesabe's two tagging boxes: one for sticky tags and one for one-time tags.

SUGGESTIONS: THE MORE, THE BETTER

When it comes to making suggestions, the operating principle seems to be "the more, the better." Here are two examples.

Del.icio.us' offers three kinds of suggestions but gives users access to recommended tags first, their own tags second, and popular tags last. Del.icio.us also uses color to help you pick tags you've used before from the recommended and popular tags.

Amazon.com uses two kinds of suggestions—an autosuggest box that shows you popular tags while you type (along with how many times the tag has been used). It also offers a list of popular tags *for that resource* with check boxes beside them. You can tag the book or DVD simply by clicking the box beside the tags you want. See **Figure 6.9**.

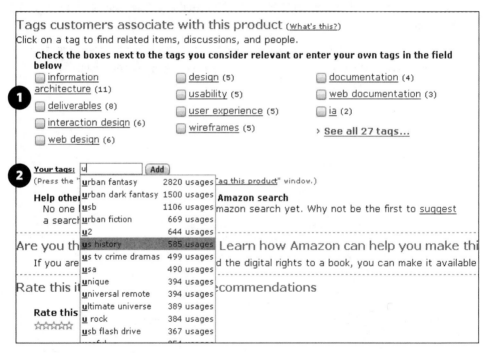

Figure 6.9 Amazon.com's suggestion interface mixes two kinds of suggestions: (1) popular tags for this book are shown with check boxes beside them, and (2) an autosuggest feature shows you popular tags based on what you've typed.

The tensions we discussed in Chapter 1—between personal versus social use of the system and between standard and idiosyncratic tags—are apparent in these examples. Amazon.com's suggestions strongly push you toward existing tags by allowing you to tag without even typing. Although less bold, Del.icio.us's suggestions also encourage the use of certain tags.

How Valuable Are Suggestions?

Sure, suggestions can make it easier for people to add tags. But by nudging users toward existing tags, suggestions also influence people's tag choices.

Does this nudging affect the quality of tags overall by encouraging users to select existing tags instead of creating new and potentially more descriptive tags?

It depends on the reasons people are tagging in a particular tagging system. If people are tagging for personal re-findability—to mark resources just for their own future use—then suggestions based on previously used tags probably offer valuable assistance.

If people are using tags to collectively categorize resources, then selecting suggested tags could be seen as an affirmation of those collective opinions. Suggestions of popular tags would be an easy way of adding one's voice to the chorus.

When it comes to tagging's role as a distributed way of collecting descriptive metadata, however, suggestions can be problematic. This is what Marieke Guy and Emma Tonkin say in their paper "Folksonomies: Tidying up Tags?":

> There are obvious dangers in establishing a positive feedback loop where potentially unsuitable tags may be reused due to the tag's initial popularity and subsequent exposure as a tag recommendation. This leads one to wonder whether it is preferable to have popular (but perhaps not intuitively obvious) tags, or to have a larger spread of relatively uncommon tags, possibly representing more accurate reflections or a wider spread of points of view.

This is an area where you should appreciate those trade-offs. Suggestions will make tagging easier, but they may reduce the diversity, quality, and possibly even the accuracy of the tags in your system.

Ultimately, your choice of a suggestion interface should be driven by your users' needs and the goals of your tagging system. But you'll need to watch that balance between the personal, social, standard, and idiosyncratic aspects of tagging if you want to satisfy everyone.

Tag Management

Once tags are added to a resource, users need a way to manage them. Renaming and removing tags are the most basic tag management functions. Users might also need more complicated tools, such as ways of grouping and splitting tags.

Like with other metadata, the value of tags will be limited if they're inaccurate or out-of-date. In fact, inaccurate tags might actually hurt tag navigation and searching (though it's important to remember that future retrieval is just one motivation for people who tag).

Users themselves will have different needs when it comes to managing their tags. Some may be tag gardeners who enjoy pruning and weeding their tags regularly to keep them organized. Others may be quite happy to let their tags grow, adopting new ones and abandoning the old without giving much thought to the whole collection. (Most people probably fall into this latter group, a point we'll discuss in just a moment.)

Editing and Deleting Tags

When it comes to managing their tags, the most basic tasks users will need to perform are editing and deleting tags.

This could mean anything from fixing a misspelled name to removing tags that have become inaccurate (for example, you might want to remove the "toread" tag after you've gotten around to reading that document).

The simplest form of tag editing can be called *re-tagging*. In Del.icio.us, users edit the tags they applied to a bookmark by simply re-tagging the item. Flickr users can also delete a tag and then re-tag the photo.

Batch Editing and Splitting

This works well when you're editing a single resource, but what about changing multiple resources or tags at once? People usually accumulate so many bookmarks or photos that editing tags one by one would be tedious, if not impossible.

A tagging system doesn't need to be very large before it makes sense to offer editing and deleting for groups of tags together. Batch editing and deleting is like a global find and replace for your tags—it changes or removes every instance of a tag across your entire collection of resources.

Most of the tagging systems that have this option also let you replace one tag with two or more new tags—effectively splitting the tag into multiple new tags. See **Figure 6.10**.

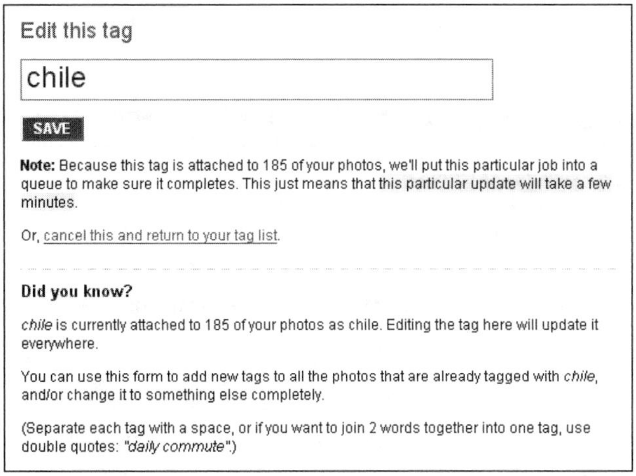

Figure 6.10 shows an "Edit this tag" interface with the following content:

> **Edit this tag**
>
> `chile`
>
> **SAVE**
>
> **Note:** Because this tag is attached to 185 of your photos, we'll put this particular job into a queue to make sure it completes. This just means that this particular update will take a few minutes.
>
> Or, cancel this and return to your tag list.
>
> **Did you know?**
>
> *chile* is currently attached to 185 of your photos as chile. Editing the tag here will update it everywhere.
>
> You can use this form to add new tags to all the photos that are already tagged with *chile*, and/or change it to something else completely.
>
> (Separate each tag with a space, or if you want to join 2 words together into one tag, use double quotes: *"daily commute".*)

Figure 6.10 Editing and splitting tags in Flickr.

This hints at more sophisticated tag management techniques. For example, a system could offer conditional splitting, where the user can replace all their tags that matched a certain criteria with a new tag.

But these kinds of systems have yet to emerge. You would think that an interface streamlined for getting information in would need to be good at managing the information once it's entered. That's not the case with the tagging systems.

Manage or Ignore?

One reason might be that people don't manage tags the way they might manage their filing system at home. Tags that are no longer necessary, such as the ad hoc tags we talked about earlier, simply lapse into disuse. We can use the browsing and filtering interfaces discussed in the previous chapter to filter out our unused and off-the-cuff tags. In short, it may be easier to ignore some tags than to manage them.

This runs counter to our information management sensibilities. We've been cultured to think of one-off and stale categories as problems. But when it comes to tags, they may simply be products of living in the stream (our metaphor for ubiquitous information flow introduced in Chapter 1).

In the stream, the volume and pace of information we encounter precludes comprehensive management. We may simply tag for now, and if a piece of information proves to be valuable later, we might put it into a folder or a browser bookmark or some more manageable structure. Until then, we have it loosely tethered with one or more tags.

Tim Spalding: Moderating Tags in LibraryThing for Libraries

An interview with Tim Spalding, the founder of LibraryThing.

LibraryThing for Libraries is a service public libraries can use to augment their online catalogs with tags from LibraryThing. It's notable because the tags are moderated—not all the tags that appear on LibraryThing are included in the data shared with libraries.

How do you exclude tags from LibraryThing for Libraries?

First we set a lower level—a tag has to used by five people 15 times. Second, we actually went through them. We thought of opening this up to the users, but basically our idea was that we're going to be very loosey-goosey on the Web site. But libraries want to have certain assurances about this stuff. So we actually had a librarian go through and say "yes" or "no" to 25,000 tags.

We went through tags that are clearly ambiguous, tags that are personal. We also went through and gave movie ratings to the naughty tags so "sex" is R and "bdsm" is X. Libraries, if they want to, can choose to screen that stuff out.

It's interesting how your approach to moderation differs depending where people are coming from.

Libraries have a very different risk tolerance. You take something like *The Diary of Anne Frank* that has 7,000 tags. Not one of them is anti-Semitic. But someday, someone is going to add an anti-Semitic tag to it. That's going to be OK [in LibraryThing] because statistically it will wash out, but in a library catalog I'm not sure that's going to be OK.

Do you see libraries picking up tagging?

There's all these OPAC [Online Public Access Catalog, the software that libraries use to put their catalogs on the Web] vendors who are doing tagging, and all of them are thinking of it as a feature. They're imagining that suddenly they'll introduce it, and it will be useful. I don't think people are that incentivized to tag in a library context. And they're surely not incentivized to tag when it's like a desert.

Everything about tags that works, works better when there's a large volume. And everything that is wrong about tags is mitigated by having a large volume.

Summary

- Tagging interfaces mix two patterns: one based on the action the user is performing (*adding and tagging* or *just tagging*) and another based on the number of resource she's acting on (*one or many*).

- Tagging interfaces are characterized by speed and simplicity. They typically involve entering multiple tags at once (a character-delimited system) or one tag at a time (an action-delimited system).

- Some tagging systems use suggestions to accelerate the tagging process. Suggestions can be previously used tags, popular tags from other users, or recommended tags (based on some other algorithm).

- Tag management interfaces let users edit, delete, and even split their tags. But really, managing tags has received little attention because it may be easier to ignore out-of-date and out-of-fashion tags than to manage them.

7 Technical Design

WHAT YOU'LL LEARN IN THIS CHAPTER:

■ Creating your tagging database

■ Displaying tag clouds with proportional and linear scaling

■ Using FreeTag, an open-source tagging plug-in for PHP and MySQL

■ Creating a tag suggestions interface using FreeTag and Ajax

In this chapter, you'll learn how to design the back end of a tagging system. Databases, SQL queries, and PHP scripts will be discussed (and linked to material covered in other chapters).

The goal of this chapter is to get developers on the same page as designers and information architects, and it's written with the Web developer in mind. However, it's not meant to be an in-depth discussion of everything technical about tagging. The examples here are straight-forward; they're more like illustrations in code than production-ready scripts. They assume some familiarity with Web programming and databases—no "Hello, world!" here.

All examples are in PHP, but you should be able to translate them easily to Ruby, C#, or your favorite programming language. By the end of the chapter you'll understand the basic technical design of a tagging system, and you should be able to start creating your own system right away.

Data Models

One of the first things you'll need to do is set up a database to store tags, users, resources, and other data you'll need for your system.

Any relational database will do the job. You could choose Microsoft Access or SQL Server, Oracle, or the open-source MySQL database. The data models and queries in this chapter were tested with MySQL 5; however, they should work with just about any database with adjustments.

You'll learn about two data models in this section: one for a simple tagging system and one for a collaborative tagging system. The data models themselves are generic, which means you can apply them to a wide variety of situations. On the other hand, you'll need to modify them to fit your particular needs. If you have an application for tagging movies, you'll obviously need different fields than someone who has an application for tagging cars.

Let's review the data modeling convention used in this chapter. **Figure 7.1** shows a basic entity relationship diagram with two entities (the parent table and child table) and the relationship between them (a one-to-many relationship).

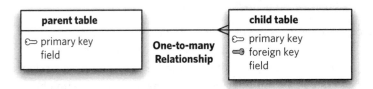

Figure 7.1 A basic data model. The white key icon indicates a primary key, and the gray key icon indicates a foreign key.

Each box represents a table. The name of the table is in bold at the top, and its fields are listed underneath. The one-to-many relationship means that for every record in the parent table there are one or more records in the child table. The connection between records is tracked through the keys; specifically, the primary key from the parent table is stored in the foreign key field in the child table.

If you've done any Web programming, you're probably already familiar with these concepts, even if you haven't used this notation.

Simple Tagging Model

Let's start first by considering a very simple tagging system where users will tag some existing resource for their personal use. This is a system that's well-suited for personal information management applications—such as tagging e-mail, for example.

In this example, each user has multiple resources; each resource is unique to each user; and each resource has multiple tags. There's no collaborative tagging here.

This system involves four database tables. There are tables for **users**, **resources**, and **tags**. To keep your database normalized, an intermediary table called **resources_tags** will keep track of which tags are applied to which resources.

The data model for this system will look like the one in in **Figure 7.2**.

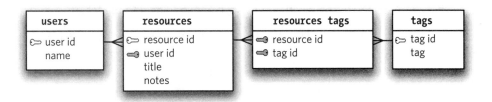

Figure 7.2 Data model for a simple tagging system.

Extracting data from this database is elementary. **Script 7.1** shows a SQL statement for selecting tags for a single resource. (In this and other SQL examples, you'll follow the convention of making table names lowercase and separating words with underscores.)

Script 7.1 A SQL statement for selecting a list of tags applied to one resource

```
SELECT tag
FROM resources_tags
  INNER JOIN tags ON resources_tags.tag_id = tags.tag_id
WHERE resources_tags.resource_id = 1
```

If you want to create a tag cloud, you can use SQL's **COUNT** function to extract the number of times each tag has been entered for any given user. In **Script 7.2** you'll ask the database to return every tag and a count of how often it has been used for **user_id = 1**. This example also uses table aliases to make the queries shorter and easier to understand.

Script 7.2 Selecting a list of tags with their frequency count

```
SELECT t.tag, COUNT(t.tag_id) AS tag_count
FROM resources r
    INNER JOIN resources_tags rt ON r.resource_id = rt.resource_id
    INNER JOIN tags t ON rt.tag_id = t.tag_id
    INNER JOIN users u ON r.user_id = u.user_id
GROUP BY t.tag, u.user_id
HAVING u.user_id = 1
```

You'll learn how to convert the results of this query to a tag cloud a bit later in this chapter.

Inserting data into this database is also straightforward. You will need to watch the usual rules around normalization—every tag in the **tags** table must be unique, which means checking each tag to see whether it exists before adding it to the table.

This kind of tagging system would be suitable for personal information management applications, but it doesn't allow shared resources or collaborative tagging. For a collaborative tagging system, you'll need to expand your data model.

Collaborative Tagging Model

Collaborative tagging requires you to track the relationships between the three core pieces of your tagging system:

- Users
- Tags
- Resources

This requires a minor change to the database previously described but one that has significant implications. To switch to a collaborative tagging model, you drop the table **resources_tags** and add a new intermediary table called **users_resources_tags**.

This new table allows multiple users to tag the same resource—the essence of collaborative tagging. It stores the user, resource, and tag IDs every time a resource is tagged. A resource with three tags will require three entries in **users_resources_tags**. This may seem like a lot of data, but in most cases it won't be a problem.

Figure 7.3 shows the data model for your collaborative tagging system.

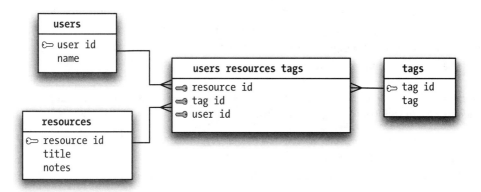

Figure 7.3 The data model for a collaborative tagging system.

The table **users_resources_tags** does a lot of work in this tagging system. It's what makes possible folksonomies, pivot browsing, and the other good things that come with collaborative tagging.

You'll have to follow the usual normalization conventions when adding data to this database. Every record in the tables **users**, **resources**, and **tags** should be unique.

Let's look at how you would access data from this database. To look up all of a user's tags (including a count), you would use the query shown in **Script 7.3**.

Script 7.3 Retrieving one user's tags in a collaborative tagging system

```
SELECT tag, COUNT(*) AS tag_count
FROM users_resources_tags urt, tags t
WHERE urt.user_id = 1 AND t.tag_id = urt.tag_id
GROUP BY tag
```

Getting a list of the most popular tags for a tag cloud is also quite easy, as shown in **Script 7.4**.

Script 7.4 Selecting the 150 most popular tags in a collaborative tagging system

```
SELECT tag, COUNT(*) AS tag_count
FROM users_resources_tags urt, tags t
WHERE t.tag_id = urt.tag_id
GROUP BY tag
ORDER BY tag_count DESC
LIMIT 150
```

Your queries will start to get more complicated when you want to do something like find the complete tagging history for a resource. **Script 7.5** shows a query that will return a list of users who tagged a resource, along with a comma-delimited list of the tags they used for that resource.

Script 7.5 Using MySQL's **GROUP_CONCAT** function to return a list of users and a comma-delimited list of their tags for a single resource

```
SELECT users.user_name, GROUP_CONCAT( tags.tag ) AS tag_list
FROM users_resources_tags urt
INNER JOIN resources ON resources.resource_id = urt.resource_id
INNER JOIN users ON users.user_id = urt.user_id
INNER JOIN tags ON tags.tag_id = urt.tag_id
WHERE resources.resource_id =1
GROUP BY users.user_name
```

In Chapter 5 you learned to combine two or more tags to filter resources. You can adjust your SQL statement to look up tag combinations—although this is not for the faint of heart.

Script 7.6 shows a query that returns a list of resource IDs and the number of users who have tagged them for a combination of three tags. It works by recursively joining the **users_resources_tags** table to find the resources that have all three of the tags you want.

Script 7.6 Finding all resources tagged with "design" and "blog" and "web"

```
SELECT DISTINCT urt3.resource_id, COUNT( DISTINCT urt3.user_id ) AS user_
count
FROM tags t1 CROSS JOIN tags t2 CROSS JOIN tags t3
INNER JOIN users_resources_tags urt1 ON t1.tag_id = urt1.tag_id
INNER JOIN users_resources_tags urt2 ON urt1.resource_id = urt2.resource_id
AND urt2.tag_id = t2.tag_id
INNER JOIN users_resources_tags urt3 ON urt2.resource_id = urt3.resource_id
AND urt3.tag_id = t3.tag_id
WHERE t1.tag = 'design' AND t2.tag = 'blog' AND t3.tag = 'Web'
GROUP BY urt3.resource_id
```

Ideally your tagging system will support tag combinations for an arbitrary number of tags. That means you'll have to generate the query in Script 7.6 programmatically based on the number of tags entered by your user.

The original version of this query appears on the MySQLForge wiki's TagSchema page (http://forge.mysql.com/wiki/TagSchema). I modified it slightly and changed the field names to fit with the other examples in the book. This page is an excellent resource for other tag system data models, as well as additional data access patterns, notes on database optimization, and other helpful advice.

Tag Clouds

In the discussion of tag clouds in Chapter 5, you learned two ways of scaling the text size in a tag cloud: proportional scaling and linear scaling.

With proportional scaling, the text size is proportional to the number of times a tag has been used. For tag sets that follow the power-law curve—as many of them do— proportional scaling results in a few very large tags and many small tags. Linear scaling, on the other hand, smooths out the power-law curve.

In the following sections, you'll see some code samples for doing both kinds of scaling. You'll also learn another scaling technique you can use when the other two don't work well.

Regardless of which method you choose, all your scaling examples will involve three steps:

- Picking the maximum and minimum text sizes for your interface
- Querying the database for your tags and the frequency counts
- Writing some code to convert the tag counts from the database into the text sizes you want

Proportional Scaling

Proportional scaling uses simple algebra to convert the frequency count for each tag into a text size used for display. The text size will be directly proportional to the frequency count, which is why it's called proportional scaling.

To create any kind of tag cloud, you'll need to define the smallest and largest text sizes for your cloud. You could omit this step, but then you'd probably have a mix of huge and tiny tags (as you learned in Chapter 5), and that would make for a distracting and hard-to-use interface.

In this example, you'll use a minimum size of 12 pixels and a maximum size of 48 pixels. You could also use a base size of 100 percent and a maximum size of 300 percent. (You can work in whatever units you like.)

To start, you will also need a list of tags and the frequency count for each tag. The query you used in Script 7.4 will return such a list of tags and their frequency counts. From this you'll find the tag that occurs the most often and the tag that occurs the least often.

You now have the five variables you need for scaling your tag cloud:

■ **Base**. Your smallest text size, which in this example is 12 pixels.

■ **Range**. Your largest text size minus your smallest text size. This equals 48 minus 12, or 36.

■ **Count**. The frequency count for each tag.

■ **Max**. The frequency count for the most popular tag.

■ **Min**. The frequency count for the least popular tag.

With these five variables we can define a scaling formula:

tag size = (count - min) x (range / max - min) + base

This formula will convert the tag counts from the database to a proportional value between your maximum and minimum font sizes.

In **Script 7.7** you will query tags from the database and scale them based on this formula. Script 7.7 works like this:

■ Retrieve the top 150 tags from the database.

■ Place the tags into an associative array, with the tag name as the key and the count as the value. This lets you retrieve the **max** and **min** values from the array, which are needed for the scaling formula.

■ Sort the array so that the tags will be displayed alphabetically.

■ Apply the scaling formula while displaying the tags.

Script 7.7 Creating a tag cloud through proportional scaling

```php
<?php
// Database variables
$db_host = "yourhost.yourdomain.com";
$db_user = "username";
$db_pass = "password";
$db_name = "yourdatabase";

// Connect to database
$con = mysql_connect($db_host,$db_user,$db_pass);
if (!$con) {
        die ('Could not establish connection. (' . mysql_error() . ')');
}
mysql_select_db($db_name) or die("Could not select database");

// SQL from Script 7.4
$query = " SELECT tag, COUNT(*) AS tag_count "
. " FROM users_resources_tags urt, tags t "
. " WHERE t.tag_id = urt.tag_id "
. " GROUP BY tag ORDER BY tag_count DESC LIMIT 150";
$data = mysql_query($query);

// Loop through database results and put them into a tags array
$tags = array();
while($row = mysql_fetch_array($data)) {
        $tags[$row['tag']] = $row['tag_count'];
}
//Sort the array alphabetically
ksort($tags);

// Set variables for tag cloud calculations
$range = 36;
$base = 12;
$max = max($tags);
$min = min($tags);

// Loop through tags, calculate sizes and display
foreach ($tags as $tag => $count) {
```

```
        $size = round(($count - $min) * ($range /($max - $min)) + $base);
        echo "<span style=\"font-size:" . $size . "px;\">";
        echo $tag;
        echo "</span>";
}

// Close database connection
mysql_close($con);
?>
```

Script 7.7 creates a tag cloud similar to the one you saw in Figure 5.3 in Chapter 5.

Linear Scaling

When your tag frequency follows the power-law curve, linear scaling can help make the differences between tags seem less extreme. In fact, linear scaling will flatten the curve, which explains the name.

Logarithms are the mathematical magic behind linear scaling. A full discussion of logarithms is beyond the scope of this book, but the simplest explanation is that linear scaling compresses the frequency counts so that they're evenly—instead of exponentially—distributed.

In this example, the database will perform the logarithm operation rather than PHP. There are two potential benefits to this approach:

- First, databases tend to be faster than server-side scripts.

- Second, the formula you used in the previous proportional scaling example will work perfectly well in this example.

The SQL query from Script 7.4 will have to change so that it returns the logarithm of the frequency count instead of the raw frequency count. You'll use MySQL's LOG() function to do the computation.

Note

Most databases have a logarithm function; MySQL has three. In most cases it won't matter which you choose.

The SQL statement from Script 7.4 would then become the statement in **Script 7.8**.

Script 7.8 A modified query that returns a logarithm of the tag count

```
SELECT tag, LOG(COUNT(*)) AS tag_count
FROM users_resources_tags, tags
WHERE t.tag_id = urt.tag_id
GROUP BY tag
ORDER BY tag_count DESC
LIMIT 150
```

As shown in **Script 7.9**, you can use the same scaling formula you used in Script 7.7 on this data to determine the text size for each tag.

Script 7.9 Creating a tag cloud with linear scaling

```php
<?php

// Connect to database
// Query for tags
$query = " SELECT tag, LOG(COUNT( * )) AS tag_count "
. " FROM users_resources_tags, tags "
. " WHERE t.tag_id = urt.tag_id "
. " GROUP BY tag "
. " ORDER BY tag ASC LIMIT 150";

$data = mysql_query($query);

// Loop through database results and put them into a tag array
$tags = array();
while($row = mysql_fetch_array($data)) {
        $tags[$row['tag']] = $row['tag_count'];
}

// Set variables for tag cloud calculations
$range = 36;
$base = 12;
$max = max($tags);
$min = min($tags);
```

```
// Loop through tags, calculate sizes and display
foreach ($tags as $tag => $count) {
        $size = round(($count - $min) * ($range /($max - $min)) + $base);
        echo "<span style=\"font-size:" . $size . "px;\">";
        echo $tag;
        echo "</span>";
}

// Close database connection
mysql_close($con);


?>
```

This script produces a tag cloud like the one in Chapter 5's Figure 5.4.

How can you use the same scaling formula but get a different tag cloud? The scaling is based on the results of the LOG() function, which has made the differences in frequency count less extreme.

Table 7.1 shows five tags, their tag counts, and their sizes using the two scaling methods. As you can see from the last column, tags with moderate frequency will be larger using linear scaling—sometimes as much as 50 percent. This is the lifting-the-middle effect covered in Chapter 5.

Table 7.1 Comparing Tag Sizes Using Two Scaling Methods

Tag	Count	Size (Direct)	LOG (Count)	Size (Linear)
"Design"	120	48	4.78	48
"Web2.0"	43	24	3.76	38
"Business"	34	22	3.52	36
"Culture"	12	15	2.48	26
"Lists"	4	12	1.39	15

Before you conclude that linear scaling is always better, here's a brief warning: you should understand how tags are distributed in your system before selecting a scaling method. Download some data from your database, drop it into your favorite spreadsheet program, and create some graphs.

If your tagging patterns are irregular and you're not happy with the results of either of the scaling methods you've learned, there's another technique: class scaling.

Class Scaling

Class scaling will turn even the most irregular set of tags into a perfectly usable tag cloud. Just as the name implies, class scaling involves dividing your tag cloud into two, three, or more classes based on how frequently tags occur. But instead of formulas or algorithms, you'll be using the eyeball method to determine the number of classes and the class sizes.

Of course, you'll want to consider the trade-offs, such as legibility and accuracy, as you learned in Chapter 5. Your main objective is to pick a handful of classes and determine how to size them so that they're attractive and usable.

With the tools you've learned in this chapter, you should have no problem figuring out class scaling. I'll leave this as an exercise for you to do on your own time.

FreeTag

FreeTag is a simple, open-source tagging plug-in that lets you add tagging functionality to just about any application. Gordon Luk, a Web developer with Yahoo, created FreeTag in 2004.

Rather than developing a particular kind of tagging application, Luk created a generic add-on that could extend other systems. Dozens of applications use FreeTag, including the popular event-planning Web site Upcoming.

FreeTag is written for PHP 4 and MySQL, and it can be used with any application that stores resource and user IDs as integers.

FreeTag also extends the collaborative tagging model discussed previously in this chapter in some interesting and useful ways. For the next few examples, you'll learn a collaborative tagging system that uses FreeTag as the tagging engine.

FreeTag Basics

FreeTag works with existing MySQL databases, so let's assume you already have tables in your database for users and resources. When you install FreeTag, You'll have two additional tables: `freetags` and `freetagged_objects`.

Your database will look like something like **Figure 7.4**.

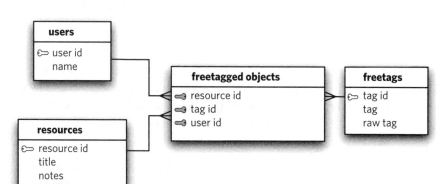

Figure 7.4 FreeTag installs two additional tables (FreetaggedObjects and Freetags) to a database.

FreeTag's nomenclature is slightly different from what you've been using. It calls resources *objects* and users *taggers*. The concepts are the same, even if the words are different.

Notice that your database is now set up much like the one you learned about in the collaborative tagging model shown in Figure 7.3. However, FreeTag adds two extra fields:

- The original version of a tag is stored in the field **tag_raw**. A normalized version of the tag—the raw tag stripped of spaces and punctuation—is stored in the field **tags**. This allows FreeTag to accept multiword tags such as "web design."

- In the table **freetagged_objects**, each record is time-stamped (**tagged_on**) so that tags can be filtered by date.

FreeTag includes a PHP class with methods for adding, deleting, and accessing tags. Useful features such as finding related tags are also bundled with FreeTag.

But the main benefit of FreeTag is that it does virtually all the grunt work for you. You can forget about the recursive self-joins you learned previously in this chapter and focus on building a useful tagging application.

Once you've set up a database, the FreeTag API lets you start tagging quickly. **Script 7.10** shows how straightforward adding tags is—simply create an instance of the FreeTag object, tell it some details about your database, and then call the **tag_object** method.

Script 7.10 Adding tags with FreeTag

```php
<?php
// Include FreeTag PHP Class
require_once("/path/to/freetag.class.php");

// Set FreeTag Options
$freetag_options = array(
        'db_user' => "username",
        'db_pass' => "password",
        'db_host' => "yourhost.yourdomain.com",
        'db_name' => "yourdatabase"
        );

// New FreeTag object
$freetag = new freetag($freetag_options);

// Define tag variables
$user_id = 1;
$resource_id = 1;
$tags = "book web2.0 design tagging collaboration software";

// Add tags
$freetag->tag_object($user_id, $resource_id, $tags);
?>
```

When you call **tag_object**, you pass it a user ID, a resource ID, and a list of tags. FreeTag parses the tags string using spaces as the delimiter. Multiword tags in quotes are treated as one tag. It checks the database for duplicates of the raw tag. If no duplicates exist, it saves the raw tag and normalized tag as new records in the **freetags** table. The **tag_id**, **user_id**, and **resource_id** are then saved in the **freetagged_objects** table.

The great thing about FreeTag is that it's resource- and user-agnostic. It can be used for any tagging application imaginable. As long as you can pass it a **user_id** and a **resource_id**, it will work.

FreeTag Clouds

FreeTag also makes it easy to get tags out of your database, including a method that automatically generates a tag cloud for display on your Web site. Calling the method, **get_tag_cloud_html**, requires defining some basic parameters, including the number of tags in the tag cloud, the range of font sizes, CSS classes, and URLs for the tags.

But as **Script 7.11** shows, you don't have to worry about the math involved in calculating tag sizes with this method.

Script 7.11 Creating a tag cloud with Freetag

```php
<?php
// Create instance of FreeTag object

// Create tag cloud
// Set the number of tags to return
$num_tags = 100;

// Set the minimum font size in the tag cloud
$min = 10;

// Set the maximum font size in the tag cloud
$max = 20;

// Set the font size units
$units = "px";

// Set the CSS class for the span
$css_class = "tag";

// Set the URL that each tag will link to
$url = "tag.php?tag=";

// Generate tag cloud
echo $freetag->get_tag_cloud_html($num_tags,$min,$max,$units,$css_class,$url);
?>
```

For each tag in your tag cloud, FreeTag generates the following code based on your parameters:

```
<span class="tags" style="font-size:20px;"><a href="tags.
php?tag=design">design</a></span>
```

FreeTag uses a proportional scaling for its tag clouds. Because it's an open-source tool, you could modify it to use another scaling approach.

Suggestions Using FreeTag and Ajax

Let's ramp up the learning curve for one final example. In this script, you'll use FreeTag and Ajax to generate tag suggestions.

This will be a basic suggestion system that shows the user tags based on their previous tagging history. Here's how it will work: the user will type some tags into an input field. When they type a space—signifying the end of a tag—you'll request a list of similar tags for the tag they just typed. You'll then display those underneath the input field as links. When they click a suggestion, it will be added to the input field (see **Figure 7.5**).

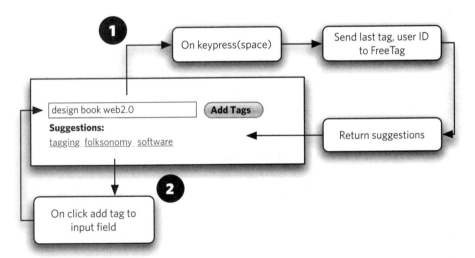

Figure 7.5 (1) After each tag is entered, an Ajax request will fetch tag suggestions from FreeTag. (2) When the user clicks a suggestion, it will be added to the input field.

To create this suggestion system, you'll call FreeTag's **similar_tags** method. This method takes a user ID and a tag and returns an array of related tags added by that user. For each tag a user enters, you want to find a list of up to 10 related tags they've previously entered.

Of course, these suggestions will be helpful only if the user sees them while they're typing—without the page reloading. To do that, you'll use Ajax to fetch your related tags without reloading the page. Ajax is a set of techniques that use JavaScript and XML to create rich interactions on Web pages.

Rather than write all the JavaScript by hand, you'll use a JavaScript framework to do some of the work for you. There are a handful of good JavaScript frameworks—such as Scriptaculous, MooTools, jQuery, and the Yahoo User Interface library—that simplify Ajax programming. You'll use jQuery in this example.

jQuery is a compact but powerful set of libraries that make Ajax and Document Object Model manipulation easy. A full introduction to jQuery would take another book, but if you understand JavaScript, you'll grasp jQuery quickly.

Note

For in-depth information about jQuery or to download the jQuery library used in this example, visit http://jquery.com.

Finally, you'll create two PHP files for your system. The first, **tags.php**, will contain your JavaScript and input form. The second, **suggestions.php**, will look up the similar tags from FreeTag and return them as XML.

Let's start with **suggestions.php**. You will pass **suggestions.php** two variables, a user ID and a tag, through an HTTP POST. The script will call FreeTag's **similar_tags** method to return an array of suggestions. You'll convert this array to XML that you can use in **tags.php**.

The XML will look like this (depending of course on the tag and user ID passed to it):

```
<suggestions>
        <tag>book</tag>
        <tag>blog</tag>
        <tag>Web2.0</tag>
...
</suggestions>
```

Most of **suggestions.php** should be familiar since it uses the FreeTag class discussed previously in this chapter. At the top of **Script 7.12** you check to see whether your two variables have been passed. And at the end you return the suggestions in XML format.

Script 7.12 Suggestions.php returns a list of related tags from Freetag in XML format.

```php
<?php
// suggestions.php

// Check for Post data
if (!isset($_POST["tag"]) && !isset($_POST["user"])) {
        die("wrong parameters");
}

require_once("/path/to/freetag.class.php");
$freetag_options = array(
        'db_user' => "username",
        'db_pass' => "password",
        'db_host' => "yourhost.yourdomain.com",
        'db_name' => "yourdatabase"
        );

$freetag = new freetag($freetag_options);

// Set parameters for similar_tags method
$num_tags = 10;
$user_id = $_POST["user"]
$tag = $_POST["tag"];

// Get array of similar tags
$suggestions = $freetag->similar_tags($tag,$num_tags,$user_id);

// Create XML of tag suggestions
$xml = "<suggestions>";

foreach($suggestions as $tag => $count) {
        $xml .= "<tag>$tag</tag>";
```

```
}
$xml .= "</suggestions>";

// Return XML
header('Content-type:text/xml');
echo $xml;
?>
```

Now you have a script that will return a list of tag suggestions in XML format.

Next let's look at the HTML for your tagging form (see **Script 7.13**). The form itself is quite simple: it has one input field with the ID "tags," one submit button, and a <div> element with the ID "suggestions."

The JavaScript you write will use the element IDs to read the tags and write back the suggestions from **suggestions.php**.

Script 7.13 The form used for entering tags

```
<form id="form" >
<input type="text" name="tags" size="50" value="" id="tags" />
<input type="submit" name="add_tags" value="Add Tags" id="add_tags">
</form>
<br />
Suggestions:
<div id="suggestions"></div>
```

With those two pieces done, you can dig into the JavaScript that makes the suggestions work. The logic for the script goes like this:

1. If the user types a space in the input field, get the last tag they typed.

2. Make an Ajax request to **suggestions.php** to get suggested tags for that last tag.

3. Loop through each of the suggested tags to make sure it hasn't already been entered in the input field.

4. Display the suggested tags as links.

5. Add a click event to each of the suggested tags so that when the user clicks the suggested tag, it's added to the input field.

That looks like it could be a lot of code, but jQuery simplifies your JavaScript significantly. jQuery scripts can be quite compact and, at first glance, hard to read. A couple of examples will make the code easier to understand:

- The $() function does most of the heavy lifting in jQuery, and it will be used throughout the script.

- The $() function can be used to fetch information from your document. For example, the expression $("#tags").val() finds the element with the ID "tags"—the input field of your form—and returns its value.

- Once you've found a document element, you can change it, add to it, and even add events to it. The expression $("#tags").click(function(){alert("Hello World!");}) adds an **onClick** event to your input field.

- In **Script 7.14** you'll see a lot of dollar signs—that's jQuery in action.

Script 7.14 Tags.php displays the suggestions as the user types

```php
<?php
// tags.php
// actually contains no PHP, just JavaScript and HTML
?>
<!DOCTYPE html PUBLIC "-//W3C//DTD XHTML 1.0 Strict//EN"
        "http://www.w3.org/TR/xhtml1/DTD/xhtml1-strict.dtd">
<html xmlns="http://www.w3.org/1999/xhtml" xml:lang="en" lang="en">
<head>
<meta http-equiv="Content-Type" content="text/html; charset=utf-8"/>
<title>Tag Suggestions</title>
<link rel="stylesheet" href="css/screen.css" type="text/css" media="screen"
/>
<script type="text/javascript" src="js/jquery.js"></script>
<script type="text/javascript">
$(document).ready(function(){

// Set the user_id. This is normally from cookie or session variable
// For this example you'll choose an existing user
var user_id = 1;

// Check for keypress event on your input field
$("#tags").keyup( function(e) {
```

```
// Conditional variable to handle IE/Firefox differences
var key = (window.event)?event.keyCode:e.keyCode;

// If user presses the space bar, display tag suggestions
if (key==32) {
        // Clear any existing suggestions
        $("#suggestions").text("");

        // Get the current tags from the input field
        var current_tags = $("#tags").val();

        // Create an array from the current tags
        var tag_array = $("#tags").val().split(" ");

        // The last tag is at the second last element of the array
        var last_tag = tag_array[tag_array.length - 2];

        // Make Ajax call to suggestions.php to look up
        // suggestions for last_tag and user_id
        $.post("suggestions.php",
        {tag:last_tag,user:user_id},
        function(xml) {

                // Loop through XML and find each element 'tag'
                $(xml).find('tag').each(function(){

                // Set show_tag, default is true (1)
                var show_tag = 1;

                // If suggestion has been added set show_tag = 0
                // So it won't be displayed
                for (i=0;i<tag_array.length - 1;i++) {
                        if (tag_array[i].search($(this).text()) > -1

) {

                        show_tag = 0;
                        }
                }
```

```
                        // Display suggestion
                        if (show_tag) {
                                $("#suggestions").append(
"<a href='#' class='tag'>" +
$(this).text() + "</a> ");
                                }
                });

                // Add click event so suggested tags are
// appended to the input field
                $("a.tag").click(function() {$("#tags").val(
$("#tags").val() + $(this).text() + " ");
                return false;
                });
});
}
});
});
    </script>
</head>

<body>
<h1>Tag Suggestions</h1>

<form id="form" >
        <input type="text" name="tags" size="50" value="" id="tags" />
        <input type="submit" name="add_tags" value="Add Tags" id="add_tags">
</form>
<br />
Suggested Tags:
<div id="suggestions"></div>

</body>
</html>
```

When the user enters a tag, the suggestions **<div>** will be populated with related tags from **suggestions.php**. The recommendations will appear every time a new tag is typed (see **Figure 7.6**).

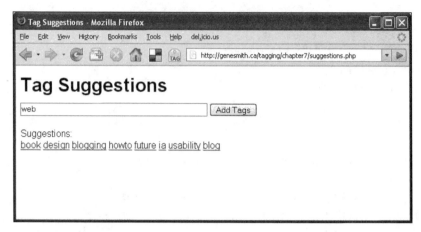

Figure 7.6 Tag suggestions for the tag "web" returned from FreeTag.

So that's it: basic tag suggestions using FreeTag and Ajax. You could extend this example by allowing the user to enter multiword tags in double quotation marks as well as single-word tags (FreeTag supports both). Or you could display a mini tag cloud of suggestions instead of a simple list.

FreeTag offers complete tagging functionality that can be plugged into almost any application (provided of course it's using PHP and MySQL).

Summary

- The data models for a simple tagging system and a collaborative tagging system are not complicated—but as you add more advanced tagging functionality, the queries can be challenging.

- Tag clouds can be created using proportional scaling or linear scaling. Proportional scaling uses each tag's frequency count to create a tag cloud, often resulting in many small tags and a few very large ones. Linear scaling uses a logarithm of the frequency count, which evens out the differences between the smallest and largest tags.

- FreeTag, an open-source tagging plug-in, can add tagging functionality to just about any kind of application. FreeTag includes helpful features, such as related tags, that can be leveraged for a tag suggestion system.

Social Bookmarking

WHAT YOU'LL LEARN IN THIS CASE STUDY:

■ A brief history of Del.icio.us, the first social bookmarking application

■ An introduction to how social bookmarking works

■ How Dogear, an enterprise social bookmarking application, got started

Tagging as we know it now began with Del.icio.us.

Del.icio.us is a social bookmarking service launched in 2003 by programmer Joshua Schachter. It was the first—and, in some ways, is still the best—example of social tagging.

Del.icio.us also launched a number of trends that would later come to be foundations of Web 2.0—like tagging, easy access to its data and services, and extending an existing technology with a social component.

This case study will give you a quick tour through Del.icio.us's history (plus a few other sites that aimed to organize the Web). We'll also look at the main features of a social bookmarking application and how they work. Finally, we'll look at how Dogear, a social bookmarking tool for large organizations, got its start.

Tip

The best way to learn about social bookmarking is to try it.
Sign up for Del.icio.us at https://secure.del.icio.us/register.

Tagging Evolution:
From Muxway to Del.icio.us

Joshua Schachter, a programmer living in New York, created Del.icio.us. Or rather, Del.icio.us evolved from a system Schachter developed for tracking—and tagging—his thousands of bookmarks.

While working on Memepool, a group Weblog he started in 1998, Schachter would collect interesting links from readers. After the bookmarks in his Web browser had overflowed, he began keeping links in a text file. To make them easier to find, he attached a keyword or two, like #wifi or #math, at the end of each URL. When he needed to track down a URL, he searched the file for one of his keywords.

Through this process, Schachter amassed some 20,000 bookmarks. He eventually built Muxway, a blog-like Web site where he published his bookmarks.

Muxway had the first implementation of tags (see **Figure A.1**). Even the name *tags* comes from a table in the Muxway database. In late 2003 Schachter created Del.icio.us (see **Figure A.2**), a more sophisticated multiuser version of Muxway.

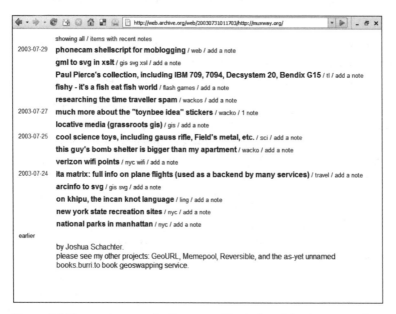

Figure A.1 Muxway is an application created by Joshua Schachter to track interesting links.

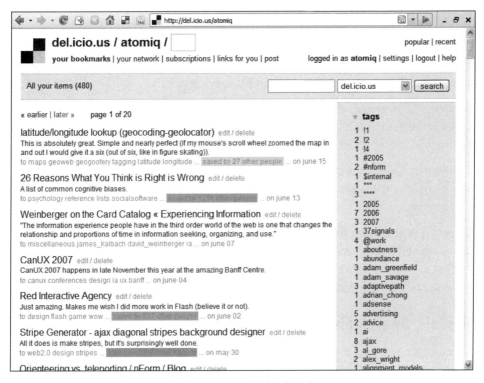

Figure A.2 Muxway evolved into Del.icio.us, a social bookmark manager.

Del.icio.us gave each user their own Muxway, but it also aggregated information from all users to show what bookmarks and tags were popular.

Schachter didn't think of Del.icio.us as a start-up, or even a business. Like Muxway or Memepool, it was an interesting side project for Schachter that complemented his days programming at a brokerage house in New York.

But people immediately began to notice something special about Del.icio.us. It was more than just a way to share bookmarks. Tags could help you discover links to topics in which you were interested.

And when you looked at everyone's tags for a particular Web page, you had a collective opinion on the subject of that page. Best of all, no one had to classify the page, place it into the "correct" folder, or identify the proper category. All that work was done by individual Del.icio.us users saving the page for their own personal use.

Del.icio.us was a personal and social utility unlike any other. It brought personal benefits—you could quickly save and tag Web pages you found interesting—while creating a loose form of community.

Organizing the Web

Del.icio.us is just the latest in a long line of applications and Web sites intent on taming some of the Web's complexity. In many ways, Del.icio.us succeeds by following the same principles as the Web itself: simplicity and openness.

Much has been written about how the Web started at the Swiss physics laboratory CERN in the early 1990s and why it succeeded. There were other hypertext systems before the Web, but none as widely (and wildly) popular.

Tim Berners-Lee used simple one-way links when creating the Web. The brilliant thing about one-way links is that they can be used to create just about any kind of organization scheme.

Berners-Lee also made the Web open—you never need permission to create a link. By nature of its openness, the Web also encourages the reorganization of documents. Almost as soon as the Web began, people began creating guides and directories to make sense of the growing tangle of links.

Portals, Search Engines, and Blogs

Yahoo began remixing the messy Web in 1994 (see **Figure A.3**). Its neatly organized categories were like the nested folders you see when you browse your hard drive or the Dewey Decimal Classification system you find at the library. Over time its collection grew to thousands of links, but it was never complete.

In the book *Founders at Work*, Yahoo's first employee, Tim Brady, explained the Yahoo directory: "We had this searchable directory. It was big, and it had all the popular sites so you could search for anything on it. But it didn't have everything. If you really wanted to search for that needle in the haystack, that wasn't us."

Other efforts to organize the Web into hierarchical categories faced the same challenge. The Open Directory project began as an open-source collaborative version of Yahoo's directory, and by any account it's a huge success. Its editors are volunteers, and it has rules for ensuring the quality of sites that it lists. It currently boasts nearly 5 million sites and 600,000 categories.

But those 5 million sites are a tiny fraction of the whole Web. By 2000 Google was already indexing nearly 2 billion Web pages, and today search engines claim to search tens of billions of pages. By indexing faster than any human-powered directory could, search engines proved to be much more effective in making the Web accessible.

Figure A.3 Yahoo started as an online directory that organized the Web into hierarchical categories.

Around the same time that search engines overtook directories, blogs emerged as a platform for people to share stories, articles, and information. Bloggers formed loose communities and traded links and commentary on various topics—from Web design to U.S. foreign policy to television to just about anything else.

Blogs brought a new dimension to finding information online. Search engines could find that needle in a haystack, and directories could give you the best sites on a particular topic. But blogs were the Web's version of word of mouth, and they were great for *social discovery*—finding things that you were interested in from people like you.

As they grew in popularity, blogs were where you would find the "good stuff"—the really interesting links you wanted to share with your friends.

In a 2004 interview posted at the blog *Rands in Repose*, Schachter drew a parallel between social discovery and the name of his nascent social bookmarking application: "In early discussions, a friend referred to finding good links as 'eating cherries' and the metaphor stuck, I guess." In 2005, Del.icio.us was purchased by Yahoo.

Online Bookmarks

Del.icio.us's success is in some ways remarkable since it wasn't the first online bookmarking application. In 1999, two former Netscape employees launched Backflip, one of several start-ups that set out to solve the same problem: keeping track of all of those links.

Backflip offered a "personal Yahoo-style directory" of folders for filing bookmarks. It used autocategorization software that attempted to automatically place bookmarks in the correct folder (with mixed success).

Backflip earned the breathless praise of many journalists during the dot-com bubble. As noted in an article posted at Traffick.com, "It may well turn out that Backflip will be the Web navigation story of 2000, just as Google blew us all away in 1999." But some already recognized the value of social bookmarking. In a January 2000 article on Backflip in *Information Week*, Gregory Smith wrote, "The missing piece is the inability… to create collaborative team folders so co-workers can browse and comment on the bookmarks of others."

After the dot-com crash, Backflip sold its technology to a group of former employees and continues to operate at http://backflip.com.

Social Bookmarking

By merging the blogosphere's social discovery with online bookmarks, Del.icio.us introduced a new category of Web application—social bookmarking. Del.icio.us has inspired dozens of imitators, many of them extending the core ideas of social bookmarking in interesting ways:

- Ma.gnolia features bookmarks and tags like Del.icio.us but also offers additional social software features such as groups.

- Connotea and CiteULike are used by scientists and researchers.

- Lotus Connections and ConnectBeam offer social bookmarking applications developed specifically for large organizations.

Despite these imitators, Del.icio.us remains the archetypal example of a social book-marking system. As you'll see in the next section, Del.icio.us still defines our under-standing of tagging and tagging systems.

How Social Bookmarking Works

Social bookmarking applications give you a place to save, tag, and share interesting links online.

Like other Web-based applications, they let you access your links from any computer connected to the Internet. Instead of saving your bookmarks in a single browser on one computer, online bookmarks make your links accessible anywhere. But the main benefit of social bookmarking applications seems to be social discovery—finding new and interesting links from other users and their tags.

Del.icio.us is the best-known social bookmarking application, so we'll use it as the start-ing point for this in-depth look at social bookmarking. We'll also consider two other sites that extend its core features: Connotea, a social bookmarking application for scientists, and Ma.gnolia, a Del.icio.us competitor.

Saving and Tagging Bookmarks

The most common use of Del.icio.us is to save and tag bookmarks. Del.icio.us book-marks (also called *posts*) are a combination of five pieces of data:

- A URL
- A description
- Notes about the URL (which are optional)
- Tags (also optional)
- A check box indicating whether the bookmark is private (optional)

Del.icio.us also tracks the date and time you submitted the resource. The three most common ways of saving a bookmark are through a Web form, a bookmarklet, or the Del.icio.us browser extension.

WEB FORMS AND BOOKMARKLETS

The most straightforward way of adding a bookmark to Del.icio.us is through its Web form. You add the URL (along with the description notes and tags), click Save, and it's added to your list of bookmarks.

Bookmarklets are small applications built into a browser bookmark that sits on the browser toolbar. Bookmarklets are really shortcuts to the form for posting URLs to Del. icio.us. But they also prepopulate some of the form fields with information about the Web page you're saving—minimizing the disruption to your browsing session.

Del.icio.us has a "post to del.icio.us" bookmarklet you can add to your browser. Clicking the bookmarklet sends the current Web page to Del.icio.us for saving and tagging (see **Figure A.4**).

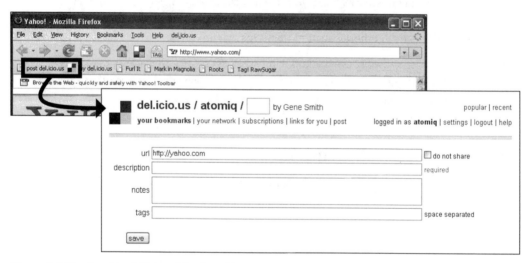

Figure A.4 The "post to del.icio.us" bookmarklet is a convenient shortcut for saving URLs.

BROWSER EXTENSIONS

Another way of adding a bookmark to Del.icio.us is through the Firefox or Internet Explorer browser extension. These extensions add icons to your browser toolbar (see **Figure A.5**) that let you save and tag the current Web page in Del.icio.us.

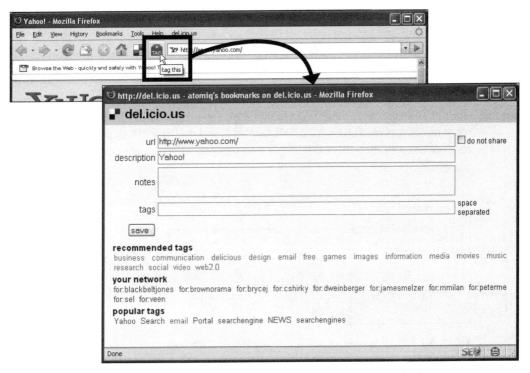

Figure A.5 The Del.icio.us browser extension adds a Tag button to the browser. The button summons a pop-up window where you can save and tag the current page.

ADDING TAGS

Whether you add a bookmark through a form, bookmarklet, or toolbar button, you'll tag the bookmark as you save it. You add tags in Del.icio.us by typing words into a single text-entry field (see **Figure A.6**).

Tags are separated by spaces, so if you want to enter multiple words as a single tag, you'll have to smashwordstogether.

tags	harrypotter book7 deathlyhallows	space separated

save

Figure A.6 Del.icio.us uses spaces to separate tags. If Harry Potter isn't added as "harrypotter," it will be split into "harry" and "potter."

The space that's used to separate tags in Del.icio.us is called a *delimiter*. Other social bookmarking systems use different delimiters, like commas or semicolons. (We'll cover delimiters in more depth in Chapter 6.)

EDITING TAGS

Del.icio.us gives you a simple way to edit and, if you want, split old tags into one or more new tags (see **Figure A.7**). This form is found on the settings page, so it's probably not used all that often. Del.icio.us also lets you delete a tag without deleting your bookmarks.

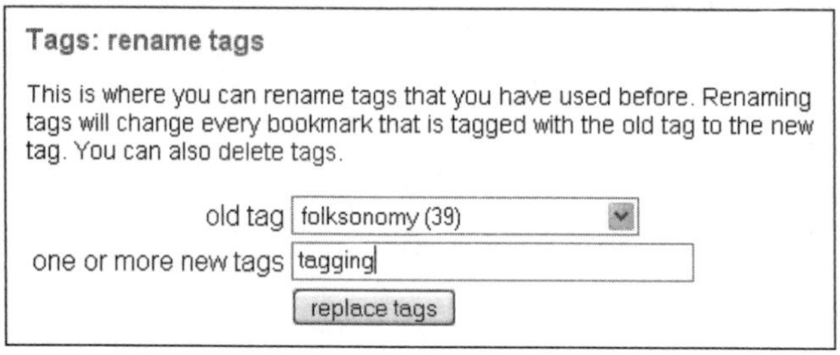

Tags: rename tags

This is where you can rename tags that you have used before. Renaming tags will change every bookmark that is tagged with the old tag to the new tag. You can also delete tags.

old tag | folksonomy (39) |

one or more new tags | tagging |

[replace tags]

Figure A.7 Renaming a tag, or splitting it into two or more tags, is quick and easy.

PULLING IN ADDITIONAL METADATA

Connotea, the social bookmarking site for scientists, can automatically discover bibliographic data when you bookmark papers from certain sources. If you save a URL from PubMed, *Nature*, *Science*, Amazon.com, or a handful of other sources, Connotea will fetch additional metadata from those sources.

This feature is important for scientists who want to use Connotea as a citation manager. Scientists build on the work of others; they revisit problems, extend methods, and reexamine theories developed by other scientists. When a scientist publishes a paper, they "pay" other scientists for their ideas by including a citation.

Connotea makes it possible for scientists to save, tag, and share bookmarks, and to track the detailed citation information they'll need when they publish their research (see **Figure A.8**).

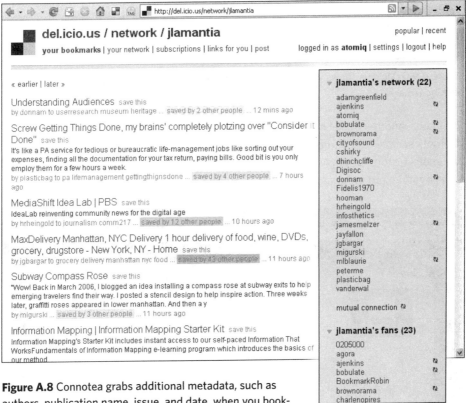

Figure A.8 Connotea grabs additional metadata, such as authors, publication name, issue, and date, when you bookmark a paper from PubMed.

Browsing Bookmarks

Del.icio.us is more than just a place to store your bookmarks. You can also use it to discover what's popular among other Del.icio.us users, track your friends' and colleagues' bookmarks, and search for popular (and unpopular) bookmarks that have been saved by others.

POPULAR BOOKMARKS

The Del.icio.us home page displays recently popular bookmarks, including helpful screen captures, and popular tags. This is a fine starting point for exploring the current interests of Del.icio.us users.

But popularity extends much more deeply. Every bookmark has a popularity indicator appended to it (see **Figure A.9**). Clicking it takes you to the posting history for that URL, which includes common tags, user notes, and a timeline of who posted it.

Analytics According to Captain Kirk edit / delete
An analysis of the mortality rate of red-shirted Enterprise crew members used to explain web
analytics.
to analytics infographics startrek ... saved by 50 other people ... 2 days ago

Figure A.9 Del.icio.us shows you how many other users saved
each bookmark.

Ma.gnolia, another social bookmarking tool, takes this feature a step further with
its Roots service (see **Figure A.10**). By clicking a Roots bookmarklet you can get the
Ma.gnolia history for any Web page, right on that page. Roots dims the page and displays a rating, top tags, and comments about the page from other Ma.gnolia users.

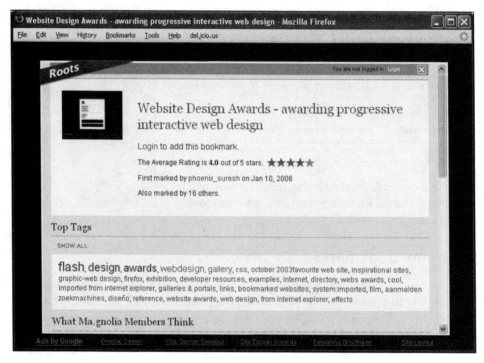

Figure A.10 Ma.gnolia's Roots gives you the bookmarking history for any page.

BROWSING AND FILTERING WITH TAGS

You can also explore Del.icio.us bookmarks through tags. Your tags help you find the bookmarks you've saved. But you can look at how other people have used a particular tag.

The folks who developed Dogear, IBM's social bookmarking tool, came up with this helpful description: "The ability to reorient the view by clicking on tags or user names, called *pivot browsing*, provides a lightweight mechanism to navigate the aggregated bookmark collection."

Del.icio.us lets you combine tags to filter bookmarks as well. You can, for example, combine "css+Webdesign" to view just the URLs that have those two tags attached. You could also combine "tutorials+photoshop+video" (see **Figure A.11**) to find one of many video how-tos for Adobe Photoshop.

Figure A.11 Del.icio.us lets you filter tags by combining them with a plus sign.

This filtering mechanism gives you tremendous resolving power when exploring Del.icio.us. You can scan the broad landscape of tags or zoom in on a specific tag combination.

FOLLOWING USERS AND TAGS

Del.icio.us has a simple social networking component that lets you subscribe to other users' bookmarks. When you add another user to your network, their public bookmarks will appear on your network page.

Notice that the social components of Del.icio.us are public by default. You can view other people's networks—who follows them and who they follow (see **Figure A.12**).

You can also subscribe to tags and even limit those to tags used by a particular author.

The tags of Del.icio.us users tend to reflect their Web-savvy interests—like "programming," "design," and "web2.0."

In contrast, some interesting tagging behaviors have emerged on Connotea because of its appeal to a specialized audience with niche interests. For example, some researchers use the names of specific genes, diseases, and scientific disciplines to tag papers. HIV, for example, is one of Connotea's more popular tags (see **Figure A.13**).

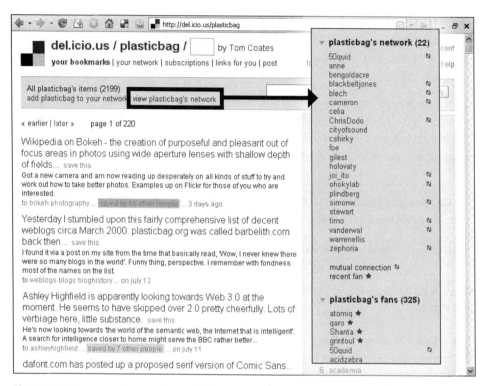

Figure A.12 You can add any other Del.icio.us user to your network. You can also view any other user's followers and fans.

AIDS ajax **and** apple Art **astronomy** Baby
bacteria **Bioinformatics** blog **blogs**
bodybuilding book Business cancer car cells
diagnosis **Drosophila** Duke duplication
evolution exercise exercises expression
fitness fmri food **Free** game **gene expression**
graph gym health HIV human **immunity**
and cancer internet Japanese java
javascript **learning libraries** lifehacks **linux**
mac **medicine metagenomics Microarray**

Figure A.13 Connotea's tag cloud showing popular scientific tags like "HIV," "FMRI," and "Drosophilia." Tags like "business" and "free" show that even science isn't immune to spam.

Extending Social Bookmarking with Web Services

Several social bookmarking sites offer an application programming interface (API) and an assortment of feeds for accessing their data. This has led to a variety of services that extract, analyze, and mash up tags and bookmarks.

FEEDS, FEEDS, FEEDS

Data feeds provide the same information on bookmarks, tags, and users as the Del. icio.us Web site, but in a format that computers can read and manipulate easily.

Every user, every tag, and even every bookmark has its own RSS feed. RSS, or Really Simple Syndication, is an XML format that many people use for sharing and consuming content. Del.icio.us will even create customized feeds for your network and your tag subscriptions. The proliferation of RSS feeds is another way of tracking the users, resources, and tags that interest you.

In addition to RSS, Del.icio.us provides data feeds in JavaScript Object Notation (JSON) and HTML format. Because all of these formats are machine-readable, they can be incorporated into other desktop and Web applications.

Terrell Russell's Cloudalicious (http://cloudalicio.us) uses Del.icio.us data feeds to graph the tagging history of bookmarks. Cloudalicious illustrates an interesting property of tagging in Del.icio.us: after a relatively small number of taggers, tags tend to reach stable proportions (see **Figure A.14**).

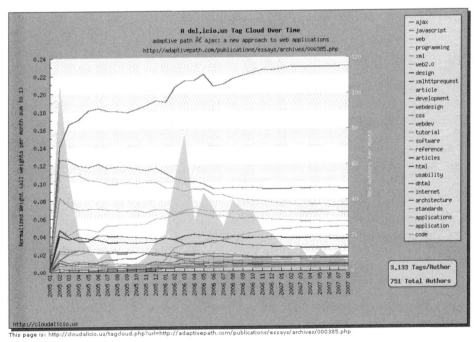

Figure A.14 A tag frequency graph created by Cloudalicio.us. Notice how the tag proportions become stable over time.

Extispicious (http://kevan.org/extispicious) is a visualization tool that generates a tag cloud from a data feed for any Del.icio.us user name (see **Figure A.15**).

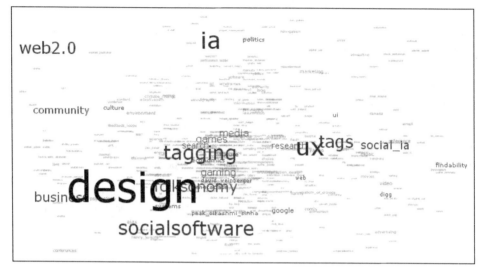

Figure A.15 A tag cloud generated by Extispicious

THE DEL.ICIO.US API

An API is a tool for developers to access the data and services on a computer. Many Web 2.0 applications like Del.icio.us, Flickr, and Google Maps offer APIs that can be used to integrate their services—like tags—into other Web and desktop programs.

The Del.icio.us API lets developers interact with Del.icio.us itself, including saving and tagging bookmarks:

- Cocoalicious and Delicer are desktop applications for managing Del.icio.us bookmarks.

- Flock, the social Web browser, integrates regular browser bookmarks with the social bookmarking services Del.icio.us and Ma.gnolia.

- Dozens of Del.icio.us-related plug-ins and scripts have been created for popular blogging platforms and browsers.

Del.icio.us's openness with its data and services has spawned a rich ecosystem of developers and applications.

But perhaps the most significant result of Del.icio.us's open-data policy is the academic research it has generated. Because Del.icio.us data is easily available, it has been the subject of dozens of formal and informal studies into tagging (many of which are referenced in this book).

This research has contributed greatly to our understanding of people's tagging patterns. In many ways, this book wouldn't be possible without that research.

David Millen: Developing Dogear, an Enterprise Social Bookmarking Application

David Millen is a group manager in the Collaborative User Experience group at IBM's T.J. Watson Research in Cambridge, Massachusetts.

Tell me about how Dogear got started.

There was some interest in social bookmarking among some of the members of my group, in particular Jonathan Fienberg and Bernard Kerr. We were aware of a number of bookmarking applications out there on the Internet, not the least of which was Del.icio.us. And we were intrigued about how they worked. We were also aware that they didn't work particularly well for the kinds of business we lived in—the very large enterprise—and they probably wouldn't work all that well for other large enterprises.

And so Jonathan and Bernard approached me in late 2004 and said, "Hey, we'd like to think about doing an enterprise version of this." I think they had the first prototype going by March 2005. And we were out on an IBM-wide trial by July.

How does an enterprise social bookmarking application differ from a consumer application?

Almost from the beginning we knew we wanted this to be behind the firewall, and that meant we needed some kind of authentication. And once you have authentication, you have in the case of Dogear real-world identity.

We weren't entirely sure how that would shape how social bookmarking would work at IBM. In the social software literature there is a role for anonymity. And we were basically not allowing that. I thought it would have some advantages. If you knew this was a bookmark belonging to, say, Jonathan Fienberg, we could link up an e-mail address, a direct link to his blog, and a direct link to his profile in our corporate directory. So we started using that real-name identity to pull in some other resources.

continued on next page

At the same time we decided we needed a mechanism to have private bookmarks. We were certainly one of the first, if not the first, to go with the notion of both public and private bookmarks. That design decision was done with quite a bit of discussion.

Social software is really quite sensitive to notions of public and private. It was my goal to keep as much in the public eye as possible to increase the sociability of the site, to increase adoption. But at the same time we thought that sometimes in an enterprise you want to bookmark things that are private. We included that, and that turned out in hindsight to have been a good decision. There is some use of private bookmarks, but not too much. So it hasn't hampered the sociability of the site.

How did people adopt Dogear?

Almost from the beginning people had a sense that this was providing an instant benefit. It started taking off first within the research group and then quite quickly within our colleagues at Lotus. We found a number of quite visible IBM bloggers who started talking about it, and then it actually started getting use beyond what we were envisioning for the first six months.

Both social bookmarking and collaborative tagging are unevenly distributed in terms of awareness and use within the company even today. Again, my belief is that this is going to continue for quite some time. Over time what I'm seeing in many aspects of social software is that there are enterprise solutions that offer the walled boundary of the enterprise—security, access control—but people also participate in these systems outside. So we're looking at ultimately how these are going to come together. And I don't mean merge together and be one thing necessarily, but there has to be ways that they play well together.

Another thing that was interesting early on was that some senior folks in IBM saw it and immediately saw the integration of bookmarks with enterprise search. Fairly early on there was a Firefox plug-in that takes a search query and queries the Dogear database and does an enterprise search and then creates a single set of results. Even that as a plug-in found a fairly wide usage. That capability is now part of the IBM enterprise search. When you query something within IBM you're going to get some Dogear results.

Can you tell me more about how social bookmarking is relevant to enterprise search?

In our case, enterprise search is hard for a variety of reasons.

The link structure in a lot of Web portals is not as rich as it is on the Internet. So some of the classic search strategies don't work as well. What you find by putting in social bookmarking is it truly is a case of the Wisdom of the Crowds. You've got pre-vetted links out there that are being indicated as being important. There's a decision of "to bookmark or not"—so that's one indicator of relevance. The second indicator is you're getting annotation for each of these—when you get end-user annotation, you're now getting a rich description of the resource. And then the final thing is the collaborative tagging, so now you've got thousands of people adding keywords. As messy as folksonomies are, that's another piece of metadata attached to that resource.

Put that all together, and that's a lot of extra information about a Web resource that a search engine can take advantage of.

How do you use Dogear to analyze social networks?

A characteristic of a social software application is that there are social relationships created in the actual fabric of the application. Now in some cases they're articulated —Friendster and Facebook do that.

Dogear is really a network based on behavior, and that's why we talk about inferring social networks based on either tag overlap or resource overlap. So there are a lot of ways you can derive that from the Dogear data. Once you've done that, it's not hard to imagine that you can now create custom recommendations—tag recommendations, resource recommendations, or even people recommendations based on some combination of resource, tag, and people. So there's a lot of value in mining this.

Part of the reason social software is so interesting to me is that in many ways that data is a by-product of the original application. It's a by-product with a huge amount of value.

One of the core research challenges is how to create an application that will sustain sociability so that you can get that by-product. It's easy to build an application that people come to once and never come back. It's hard to build one that people will continue to find value in and come back to.

IBM's Lotus division has released Dogear as part of its Lotus Connections product.

Summary

- Del.icio.us was the first application to introduce tagging as we know it. It also launched a new category of social bookmarking Web applications.

- There were other online bookmarking applications, but Del.icio.us melded the social nature of blogging and the simplicity of tagging in a successful way.

- Del.icio.us and other social bookmarking applications work well as a personal bookmarking tool, but they shine when it comes to sharing and exploring links with others.

- Social bookmarking applications have been customized for particular users (like scientists) and contexts (like large organizations).

- Del.icio.us data is easily accessible through an API or data feeds. This has spawned dozens of interesting tools, as well as vital academic research.

Media Sharing

WHAT YOU'LL LEARN IN THIS CASE STUDY:

- How tags enable object-centered sociality
- A comparison of tagging approaches at popular media-sharing Web sites
- Deep tagging and other variations on tagging videos

In this case study we'll consider the value of tags in media-sharing applications. *Media sharing* is a general term for Web sites that allow users to share photos, videos, music, and other kinds of digital media with each other.

The examples in this case study cover a broad swath of tagging systems. We have the simplest systems to full-blown collaborative tagging systems.

How Media Sharing Works

As long as we've had media, we've had people who collect and share it, from the folks who tape and trade Grateful Dead concerts to the punk rock zine scene.

Online media sharing certainly follows in the footsteps of those traditions. But in recent years it's exploded thanks to cheap storage, broadband, easily available production technologies (like digital cameras and camera phones), and online communities.

Understanding Tags for Rich Media

We've discussed the value of tagging media in other sections of the book, but it will be helpful to quickly recap the value of tagging in the media-sharing context. These applications have some challenges that are suited to tagging.

GOOD METADATA IS HARD TO FIND

Unlike Web pages, photos and videos don't come with much baked-in metadata. Search engines, for example, can typically index the contents of a Web page or other text-based format like an e-mail message, a PDF document, or a Word document. Depending on the contents of the file, they can extract different pieces of metadata, like a title, author, or creation date.

Photos and videos don't have the same advantages. For example, it's difficult for a computer program to understand that a photo of your brother Ned was taken at your sister's wedding. (Most digital cameras store EXIF, or Exchangeable Image File Format; data like the date, exposure time, aperture; and other technical details related to each photo.)

Technology is getting better at understanding rich media. For example, Riya is a photo search engine and can search for photos of people, events, and actions such as dancing. And new video search technologies use speech recognition to let you find parts of a video. But even these sophisticated algorithms would miss the context and many of the important details that surround a photo or video. This is where tags can help. Tagging is a useful and efficient way to add meaningful metadata to these kinds of files—to help make them easier to find and to ensure you can track them down when you need to do so.

OBJECT-CENTERED SOCIALITY

These media-sharing sites are also at the forefront of what has been described as *object-centered sociality*. Unlike some social networks, which focus on just the connection between individuals, media-sharing sites include an object around which social interaction occurs. The object is a piece of digital media, like a photo, video, or presentation.

The value of tags in this context is that they can connect objects together and help disparate users find each other (see **Figure B.1**). Users can have a social experience on the site without actually knowing each other because they share a common interest in a video or photo. Tags increase the social experience by helping you identify those common interests.

Figure B.1 An example of how tags can enable object-centered sociality: two users who share an interest in landscape photography discover the other's work through shared tags.

They can also let users coordinate their objects with each other, like conference attendees who add predetermined tags to their photos to create a spontaneous collection of images.

While we examine some of the features of these sites, we should keep these concepts—the need for descriptive metadata and object-oriented sociality—in mind.

Sharing Videos

The standard-bearer for online media sharing is certainly YouTube. The site features short video clips uploaded (and often created) by users. Exposure on YouTube—and across the Web through YouTube's embeddable video player—has brought Internet fame to many (just one example is the treadmill-dancing band named OK Go). It has also taken a prime spot on the political stage. In the most recent U.S. elections, a series of debates was organized around questions posed in videos uploaded to YouTube.

YOUTUBE

The remarkable thing about YouTube, at least as far this book is concerned, is how unremarkable its tags are.

In many ways, YouTube tags resemble the keywords that used to be popular on Web sites. People who created Web sites used to embed keywords in each page to improve their search engine rankings. Unfortunately, some people began using inappropriate and incorrect keywords to boost search engine traffic. As keywords became unreliable, search engines stopped indexing them altogether. (This is the metacrap problem mentioned in Chapter 4.)

YouTube's tags are added by users when they upload a video. Tags play a minimal role in YouTube's navigation (see **Figure B.2**). They aren't aggregated—there's no tag cloud—but you can search for a tag. In addition to boosting search rankings, tags are also used to retrieve related videos. When you're viewing a video on YouTube, you'll also see a list of related videos—a list based on the tags used for the current video.

Figure B.2 Tags play a smaller role at YouTube than they do on many other media-sharing sites. Clicking a tag launches a search for that term.

This is not to suggest that YouTube's tags are unreliable or even, shall we say, spammy. When you're dealing with video, every extra bit of descriptive metadata helps. But they're a supplemental form of metadata—YouTube uses channels and categories as its main browsing tools.

EMBEDDING AND EXTERNAL TAGS

Because YouTube videos can be embedded in Web pages, they can be tagged in other venues as well, like on a blog. So while tags are just one part of YouTube's *internal* navigation, they play a greater role in leading people to videos when they're embedded outside of YouTube.

For example, "video" is one of the most popular tags on blog aggregator Technorati—and most of the videos posted there are from YouTube (see **Figure B.3**).

This shows one unique feature of media sharing: resources can accumulate tags as they're shared. This is a kind of collaborative tagging system, though it happens outside of YouTube in the surrounding ecosystem of sites that embed videos.

In this situation—where the resource is shared and tagged outside of its originating site—you have an opportunity to examine how tags are used in that ecosystem. YouTube could, for example, analyze the tags used on sites that embed videos. Those tags could be aggregated, as they would in a collaborative tagging system, or they could be used to improve findability through search and browse within YouTube itself.

The point is that media-sharing applications like YouTube enjoy the benefits of tagging inside *and* outside their system.

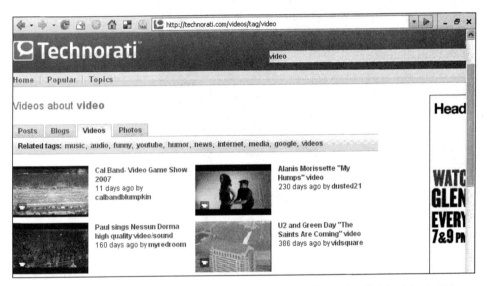

Figure B.3 Blog posts tagged with "video" on Technorati. Many of the videos link back to YouTube.

DEEP TAGGING

Deep tagging is a term for tagging a part of an audio or video file. Because these files can be quite long—it's not unusual for people to record hour-long podcasts, and movies regularly exceed two hours—jumping to a particular point in the file can be a problem. Think about watching a video of Larry King interviewing one of your favorite stars—you want to skip the questions about her latest movie (which you've seen) and get right to the part where she talks about her scandalous divorce. It's hard to find that part except by watching the whole video.

Deep tags offer a solution. Like the chapter index of a DVD, deep tags allow you to find a particular segment of a video. And just like tags, they're created by users.

Viddler is one of several companies that lets you deep-tag videos. They're called *timed tags*, and they can be added to any point on a video's timeline (see **Figure B.4**). With timed tags, the resource is not just a video but a particular time within a video file. While watching a video, you can scan the timeline to see which points have been tagged.

Figure B.4 Adding tags to the video timeline at Viddler.

Timed tags are also used to pull contextual advertising into a video. For example, a segment tagged with "guitar" might also display a small text ad for the video game *Guitar Hero*.

Viddler's approach is interesting because it allows user-generated navigation within videos. And because play, performance, and opinion tags also emerge in this context, there's an element of annotation as well.

Sharing Photos

While Flickr wasn't the first photo-sharing Web site, it was one of the first to implement tags in a way that emphasized sharing.

As you might recall from Chapter 3, Flickr is a simple social tagging system. You can give your friends permission to tag your photos—and their tags become part of your collection—but all tagging is done on what we call the *original resource*. So, Flickr never develops truly collaborative tagging for any resource.

SOCIAL COORDINATION

By aggregating tags from across users, Flickr created a simple tool for users to coordinate their photos. The focus of coordination could be an event (like a wedding), a game (like "squaredcircle"), or even something unintentional like a location.

In the book *Founders at Work*, Flickr founder Caterina Fake says, "Tagging really revolutionized the way the application behaved...you can not only see all the things that you've tagged...but you can also see what everyone else in the system has tagged themselves in the public stuff."

One of the benefits of tags to object-oriented sociality is to bring people together through their tags.

EFFICIENT INTERFACES

Flickr distinguishes itself from other sites in that it provides multiple ways of doing the same task. You can add tags from multiple places in the site—for example, while uploading a photo, while viewing a photo, and while organizing all your photos.

Flickr also makes those interfaces as efficient as possible. Let's look at two examples.

When you view a photo, you have a simple interface for entering tags—a one-line text box just like we discussed in Chapter 6 (see **Figure B.5**). Clicking in the Add box, you can type one or more tags and press Enter, and they're instantly added. The box reappears so you can continue typing, hands never leaving the keyboard, until you're done.

In fact, through judicious use of Ajax, you never have to leave this page to change any of the photo's metadata.

When it comes time to group your photos together into collections, Flickr gives you an Ajax-driven page to edit your photos in bulk (see **Figure B.6**). You can add tags to photos as a batch through this tool (though you can't split or delete tags as a batch).

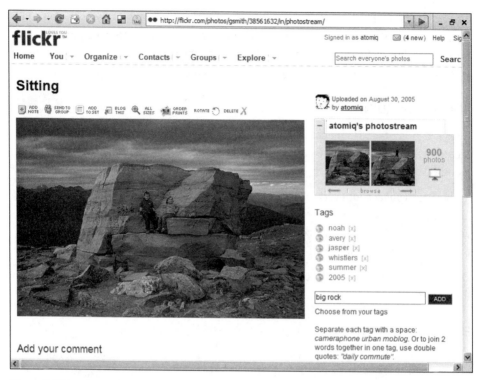

Figure B.5 Tagging a photo on the Flickr photo page. Multiple tags can be added without leaving the page.

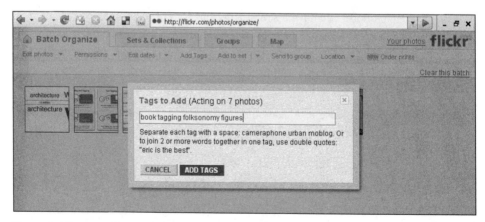

Figure B.6 Tagging photos in bulk in Flickr's Organizer.

TAGGING PHOTOS IN FACEBOOK

You can also post and tag photos on the ultra-popular social network site Facebook. Facebook is one of the most mainstream applications of tagging. But it also has adapted tagging to its goal of being a social utility that connects people.

The Facebook interface emphasizes tagging people—and in particular identifying other Facebook users in photographs. You can add other tags as well, but you're encouraged to use names.

An outcome of this approach is that you're actually tagging parts of a photo rather than just the photo itself. When you tag a photo, you click an area of the photo, and a blue box appears to identify the subject of the tag. You're then presented with the tagging interface, which includes an area for free-text tags but also has a list of your Facebook contacts (see **Figure B.7**).

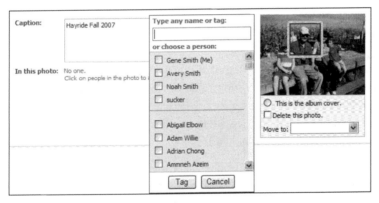

Figure B.7 Tagging in Facebook emphasizes tagging people. Note the box over the photo to identify people's faces and the use of check boxes in the tag suggestions to the left of the photo.

It's almost as if the system were designed for tagging group photos taken at parties—which wouldn't be entirely surprising since Facebook started as social network service for college students.

There is not a tag cloud to be found on Facebook (though it's always easy to find photos of yourself or of your contacts). Tags are primarily used to pull together photos of other users and to assist with search. But they're not aggregated in any other way—say to show you who appears in the most photos among your contacts.

You can recognize the tagging patterns we've discussed in this book in Facebook's tags:

■ The tags are simple, flexible, and extensible; you can enter any terms you want.

■ The tagging form is a one-line text box.

■ There are suggestions to help make the tagging process easier and more accurate.

But it's the adaptations that make Facebook's tags interesting. By focusing so strongly on tagging contacts, it's almost as if they've turned people into objects of sociality.

SlideShare

SlideShare has been called "YouTube for PowerPoint." It's a media-sharing site where you can upload and share your PowerPoint files with other users. Like YouTube, SlideShare has an embeddable player so you can post your presentations on a blog or other Web page.

Because text can be extracted from PowerPoint files, presentations don't suffer from the same metadata challenges that photos and videos do.

SlideShare has created a clever tagging system that marries aspects of Flickr and Del. icio.us. In SlideShare any other user can tag your slides as long as they mark your slides as a favorite. A favorite is just like a bookmark within SlideShare; it's a way for you to find the presentations that you like. (In the model discussed in Chapter 3, SlideShare users are tagging a pointer to the file.)

This favorites system (see **Figure B.8**) creates a collaborative tagging environment where each user has their own tags that can be aggregated for each presentation. SlideShare can then use this aggregate view to give users a sense of what each presentation is about and even which presentations are more representative for each tag.

Another interesting aspect of tagging on SlideShare is how it mixes object-centered sociality with metadata collection. According to CEO Rashmi Sinha, "Tagging/favoriting is the most popular social gesture on SlideShare."

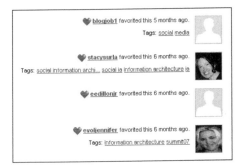

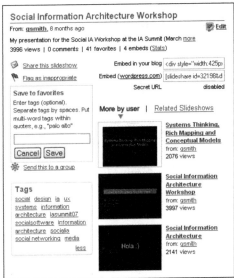

Figure B.8 SlideShare's favorites feature
mixes Del.icio.us and Flickr-style tagging.

Here's something to notice about this case study: within a fairly narrow category—
Web-based media-sharing applications—we can find just about every variation of
tagging we've discussed in this book:

- YouTube has a very simple nonsocial tagging system reminiscent of the old HTML
  keywords tag.

- Flickr offers social tagging, but not collaborative tagging.

- Viddler and Facebook give us a glimpse at more sophisticated tagging technologies
  where portions or segments of a media file are tagged.

- SlideShare provides full collaborative tagging by having users "favorite" their
  presentations and then tag them.

This diversity of tagging systems shows how much room there is to play with these
technologies and to design systems that really support your project or product.

Summary

- The need for good metadata and the principle of object-oriented sociality make tagging relevant to media-sharing sites.

- Despite a basic similarity, there can be significant differences between how media-sharing sites implement tags. YouTube's tags are like simple keywords while SlideShare uses collaborative tagging.

- Flickr lets you add tags in multiple places, and in multiple ways, emphasizing the importance of tags within its system.

- Facebook's photo-tagging system focuses on tagging people within photos, suggesting that in Facebook the people are the objects.

- SlideShare makes its tagging system collaborative with the favorites feature—similar to an internal bookmarking system.

Personal Information Management

WHAT YOU'LL LEARN IN THIS CASE STUDY:

- Two different approaches to managing online information with tags

- How tags can complement other information structures in larger PIM projects

- An in-depth look at Microsoft's Photo Gallery, a photo management application

This case study looks at tagging in the context of personal information management, or PIM. As you learned in Chapter 1, personal information management is managing your own information to get things done.

In this appendix we'll eschew the social aspects of tagging and look just at how tags can help you get organized.

Tagging for PIM

PIM applications of tagging differ from many of the others we've discussed because the social components are less important—and sometimes not important at all.

But even with the social elements removed, tagging still has benefits for organizing your information. The three main advantages of tags are as follows:

- They offer a simple, flexible, extensible categorization scheme.

- They can stand alone as a simple tool for keeping a collection of resources organized.

- They can supplement other kinds of information structures to create powerful hybrid forms of organization.

Managing Online Information

Tagging has been primarily an online phenomenon and certainly grew out of the need to manage the stream of information we increasingly encounter online. There are several online tools that use tags for information management—and to good effect. Let's look at two: Backpack and BlueOrganizer.

BACKPACK

37Signals' online PIM tool, Backpack, is a great illustration of tagging as a simple PIM tool. With Backpack, you create pages to store and organize your information—lists, notes, photos, and so on. You can tag each page, and tags can help keep groups of pages together.

In many ways, pages in Backpack are like folders. Each page can hold a variety of different kinds of things, but each thing can be part of only a single page.

In Backpack the page is the resource, so you can't tag the notes or photos within each page. Your tags can be used to aggregate your pages to navigate through your information (see **Figure C.1**).

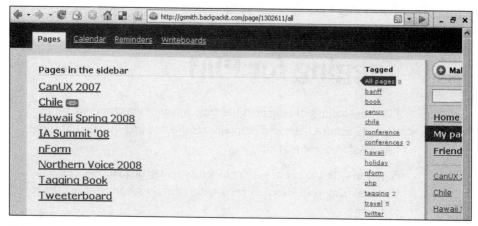

Figure C.1 You can use the tags on the right to navigate your pages.

BLUEORGANIZER

AdaptiveBlue's BlueOrganizer is a Mozilla Firefox plug-in that helps you manage book-marks. Once you've installed the plug-in, you will have a BlueOrganizer icon on your browser toolbar. Clicking the icon will bookmark the current page (BlueOrganizer calls them BlueMarks).

Up until now this sounds like a regular bookmarking application. But what distinguishes BlueOrganizer is *how* it makes tag suggestions. It uses the contents of the page you're saving to generate suggestions, and it does this in a fairly sophisticated way:

- BlueOrganizer recognizes certain kinds of information, like movies, books, and music. When you're saving a book from Amazon.com, for example, it uses the Amazon.com API to retrieve that book's categories as suggested tags (see **Figure C.2**).

- For generic pages, like a news story, it looks at how frequently words appear on the page and uses an algorithm to suggest tags from those.

- For other kinds of pages, BlueOrganizer looks for trigger words in the text (like "wine"), looks up possible tags in a dictionary, and matches them against the text on the page.

If the suggested tags aren't enough on their own, you can always add your own tags as well.

Tags are just one piece of the metadata collected by BlueOrganizer. It captures a variety of structured information for each BlueMark, depending on the kind of thing being saved (see **Figure C.2**). If you save a page from Wine.com, BlueOrganizer will extract and save the name of the wine, the winery, the grape, the region, and the year it was made (along with your tags and rating).

Figure C.2 Using BlueOrganizer to bookmark a book on Amazon.com. The tags are automatically generated by a query to Amazon.com's API, and you can add your own as well.

Managing Projects

But what about more sophisticated organization schemes? Software makers are already starting to mix tags and folders in their products. In Chapter 2 we learned that folders excel at subdividing, nesting, and categorizing information in a way that helps people understand and plan their activities. Tags can provide multiple ways to access files—rather than just a single path—and are flexible enough to capture relevant information that may not be part of the folder structure.

Milenix's MyInfo is one of several PIM applications that supports both hierarchical, and folder-like structures along with tags. MyInfo is a desktop application for the Windows operating system that can be used for a variety of PIM tasks.

Most relevant to our discussion here is how it was used to create the early drafts of this book, which required managing a strict hierarchical structure (the outline) even when there were ideas that appeared in multiple places (see **Figure C.3**).

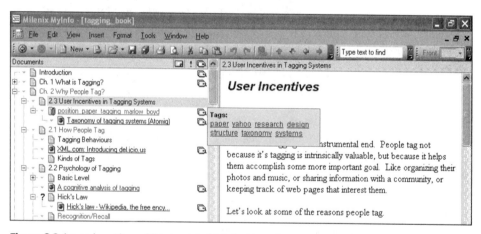

Figure C.3 An early outline of this book in MyInfo. Note the tag icon on the right of the folder list.

Here's how tags and folders worked together to keep things organized:

- Papers, links, quotes, fragments of text, and any other source materials were organized into a chapter-by-chapter outline using a folder structure. Folders were nested so that they roughly followed the headings of each chapter.

- Tags were attached to each item to identify author names, document types, and concepts that appear throughout the book. The tags could be used to aggregate chunks of information based on their shared characteristics, while keeping the outline intact.

Tags were an important tool for tracking the ideas that recur throughout the book (like the power law we discussed in Chapter 3), not just an add-on to the folder-based outline. Many large information management problems are multifaceted and thus require this kind of approach because there are usually a handful of ways to categorize any given resource.

Using Photo Gallery

Microsoft's Photo Gallery, a photo management application that ships with the Windows Vista operating system, is a good subject for the final section of this book. Photo Gallery is designed to help you manage your photos, and tags are one of the tools it uses to do that.

Photo Gallery isn't the only Windows Vista application that uses tags. You can tag just about any document right in Windows Explorer. This is one of the best examples of the evolution of tagging from exciting trend to everyday feature. What's interesting about Photo Gallery is how it has adapted tags to meet the photo management challenges of its users.

Digital cameras and cheap hard drives have changed how people take, store, and manage photos. Before you might've taken a few rolls of film on a vacation; now you can take hundreds, and it doesn't cost you any extra to keep all of them. Years ago you might've kept your unsorted photos in an old shoe box; today you keep them on a hard drive (with cryptic titles like "DSC00152").

Once again, the stream is a relevant metaphor. Many people are now creating a stream of digital photos, all waiting to be titled, labeled, tagged, and made findable. Instead of shoe boxes and photo albums, we now have programs like Photo Gallery, Apple's iPhoto, and Adobe's Photoshop Elements.

The thousands of photos we store on our computers are an information management problem. Photo Gallery has two interesting features to help you deal with this problem:

- It uses hierarchical tags, which you can assign in a nested way similar to folders.

- The tags are stored in the image itself (we called this "the truth is in the file" back in Chapter 3).

Of all the applications and Web sites we've discussed in this book, Photo Gallery is the only one with these two features.

HIERARCHICAL TAGS

Most Web-based tagging systems store tags in a flat structure, or, occasionally, tags are separated into *facets* (discussed in Chapter 4). Photo Gallery is different in that it supports hierarchical tags.

With Photo Gallery you can assign tags in a nested way similar to folders. But the interface remains simple—it's a one-line text box just like other tagging systems.

In **Figure C.4** you can see a list of tags applied to photos. You can drag and drop tags to arrange a hierarchy that works for you. Note how this is different from folders: photos can be tagged multiple times, and they can appear more than once in any tag hierarchy.

Figure C.4 On the left you can see the tag hierarchy. Selecting a tag also selects its subtags, and all the photos with those tags are displayed on the right.

The tags themselves are stored as slash-delimited strings, like "Activities/camping" or "Subjects/clouds." The hierarchies can be two, three, or more levels deep, though Figure C.4 shows only two levels.

Hierarchy allows you to create categories for your tags—you can have a tag "Places/Helena" and a tag "People/Helena" to distinguish between a person and place.

Photo Gallery uses suggestions to help mitigate the awkwardness of typing all those slashes. As you type, a number of suggestions appear based on the characters you've entered. Tags that match—regardless of where they appear in your hierarchy—are shown as suggestions.

TRUTH IN THE FILE

Another interesting feature of Photo Gallery is that it stores your tags in the image itself. This is approach is called "the truth is in the file," and it means that your tags are portable—they go wherever the image goes.

Figure C.5 shows how you can edit the tags right in a photo's Properties window. In this case you don't get suggestions or other features of Photo Gallery's interface, but you do get to see that the tags are saved with the photo.

Figure C.5 The Properties window for a photo shows you its tags. You can edit and save them, and they'll be stored in the photo itself.

While it might not seem important, there is some significance to having the truth in the file. You can e-mail a photo to someone without losing tags (or any of the other metadata you've added). You can back up a photo to another computer or a DVD and keep all your information intact.

Microsoft even released a plug-in that exports your Photo Gallery photos to Flickr, tags and all. Photo Gallery rewards your investment in tagging by making sure your metadata stays with your photos.

Scott Dart: Tagging Photos in Photo Gallery

Scott Dart is the program manager of Microsoft Photo Gallery.

Photo Gallery stores tags in a hierarchical format ("keywords/nature/animals/birds/ducks"). Why did you use this approach instead of the flat structure you typically see in tagging systems?

Anyone who has tagged their photos for any length of time will tell you that a flat list eventually becomes unwieldy. This is one of the reasons why we have hierarchical folder structures—because a flat list of folders would be too long to manage. Additionally, many organizational systems that users employ are naturally hierarchical. Tags are primarily designed to allow users to describe the subject matter of the photos—who is in the photo, where the photo was taken, what the occasion was, etc.

The nice thing about hierarchical tags is that no one has to take advantage of them if they don't need them or don't want them. As a user's photo collection and organizational system grows, they can take small steps to start taking advantage of hierarchy when they are comfortable. In the Photo Gallery, you're not locked into one organizational scheme forever; you can drag and drop tags around or combine and delete them as your needs change.

Most people end up with thousands of digital photos. Did the sheer volume of files influence your approach to tagging?

Absolutely. We've heard loud and clear from our users that they can't find their photos efficiently, even when they have only a few hundred or thousand. And digital photo collections are growing every day, so the problem is only getting worse for most people. Music is actually in a much better position, since users typically don't have to tag their music. They are able to download all of the metadata they need from their content provider. Without even having to do anything (usually), they know what album, artist, year, genre, etc., a track of music is from and can browse their music easily this way.

With photos, there is a lot of manual work involved to get to this level of organization. To compound the problem, there is typically no *one* magic bullet to photo organization. When you ask someone to find any given photo, it's hard to predict what method they will use to find that photo. It's likely to be different from one photo to the next, even for the same person. For one photo, they may recall what date it was taken (to varying degrees of specificity). For another photo, they may remember only the place it was taken. And for another photo, they are looking for a specific combination of people in the picture. Or they may want to see only their best photos (which requires rating the photo, slightly different than tagging).

Unfortunately, until recently, most users have had only one organizational tool to manage their entire collections—folders. So, they have done the best that they can with that one tool, trying to optimize for the way they find most photos and suffering when they need to find something that doesn't fit whatever system they have chosen.

It's actually not a lot of work to rate and apply multiple tags to a set of photos after you take them, but asking someone to go through their entire photographic history and do this seems like a daunting task to most people. In reality, it's not usually as hard as people expect. But who has the time or the motivation? We definitely tried to make it easy for users to tag multiple photos at once and to streamline the task of reusing the same tag over and over again. In reality, we expect users to take small steps into tagging.

Do you anticipate a time when you hide folders entirely?

Sure, but I'm not placing any bets on when that will be.

We have this discussion every year within our team (or so it seems). The answer so far has been that we don't want to take away the one tool that users have traditionally had for organizing their photos.

The real value in folders is that they are a virtual representation of where an item physically lives (on which hard disk, on which computer, etc.). In most scenarios, this is actually not very important. There are scenarios where this is needed, but those aren't primarily why users organize using folders. They do that because they have been given no viable alternative. Tagging has been around for years, but the mainstream adoption of users tagging their own photos is slow (and growing). Maybe the Photo Gallery will start to change that for some people, but there are probably some users who will never ever tag no matter how easy we make it for them.

Summary

- Tags are simple, flexible, and extensible, so they fit well into people's personal information management toolbox. But as people's PIM needs grow, tags can also work as one of a collection of tools that help to categorize, sort, filter, and find information.

- Autotagging, the approach used by BlueOrganizer, can help save people time by generating contextually relevant tag suggestions.

- Tags can also supplement a hierarchical one-thing-in-one-place organization scheme by allowing resources to be aggregated by shared characteristics instead of just location.

- Photo Gallery, a feature of Windows Vista, uses hierarchical tags to help people manage the thousands of digital photos they collect. It also saves tags in the file itself, so the tags will go wherever the photo goes.

Index